D1072306

*Printed
For
Quixote Press
by*
BRENNAN PRINTING
*100 Main Street
Deep River, Iowa 52222*
515-595-2000

FLAT-OUT, DIRT-CHEAP COOKIN' COOKBOOK

by

Bruce Carlson

* * * * * * * * *

QUIXOTE
PRESS
Bruce Carlson
R.R. #4, Box 33B
Blvd. Station
Sioux City, Iowa
51109

DEDICATION

-to Mom. For if she hadn't been able to feed me cheap, she wouldn't have been able to feed me at all.

TABLE OF CONTENTS

ACKNOWLEDGEMENTS

I would certainly like to thank all those frugal housewives who gave me good advice . . . and Amy, the world's nicest nutritionist who passed judgement on how good for you these goodies are.

I want to thank Arden, my helpful grocer who explained grocery store pricing practices on perishable goods so the snug budget can survive the shopping aisles. And, I really really have to admit that Joyce's, Terri's, Frank's, and Lou's tracking down of low cost recipies that made for good eatin' is what made this book.

Thanks a lot, all of you.

B. Carlson

PREFACE

Anyone can eat cheap if they want to do with litle, do without, use shoddy stuff, or pull in their belt.

But, if you want to eat well, enjoy your food, and still get by without it costing you an arm and a leg. . . . this is the book for you.

Now, doggone it, I went to a lot of work to pull all these recipes together, so you best buy this book!

INTRODUCTION

Bruce Carlson did it up right this time. His book FLAT-OUT, DIRT-CHEAP COOKIN' COOKBOOK is a sure-fire way to do some real good cooking without spending a lot of money.

If you've already bought this book, you made a good buy.

Professor Phil Hey
Briar Cliff College
Sioux City, Iowa

BEVERAGES

and

SNACKS

Beverages and Snacks

Divinity Candy

4 C. sugar
1 C. white Karo
1 C. water

1 C. nuts
1 tsp. vanilla
4 egg whites (beaten)

Boil sugar, Karo and water to 310° or until ther is a crackling sound when dropped in cold water. Pour slowly into beaten egg whites. Add nuts and vanilla. Continue beating until it holds shape. My mother would not make this candy on a cloudy day. There had to be sunshine and fair weather or it woild not set or harden according to her.

Aunt Ella's Oven Caramel Corn

8 or 9 qt. popped corn
2 C. brown sugar
1 C. margarine
1 tsp. salt

½ C. white syrup
1 tsp. burnt sugar or vanilla
½ tsp. soda

Mix all ingredients together, except corn and soda; boil for 5 minutes, mixing well and stirring. Remove from heat and add soda; stir in quickly and pour over popped corn, mixing well. Put in 2 large flat pans and place in 250° for 1 hour, stirring 2 or 3 times. Store in tightly closed container.

Popcorn Balls

¾ C. white corn syrup
¼ C. honey
½ C. butter
2 tsp. vinegar

1 tsp. vanilla
1½ C. sugar
6-7 qt. popped corn

Boil corn syrup, honey, butter, vinegar and sugar until it snaps or to the hard boil stage when tested in cold water. Pour over popped corn which has been heated in the oven at 250°. Mix well and form into balls, using damp hands to form the balls.

Squashed Snacks

2 C. flour
2 sticks (½ lb. ea.) soft butter
1/8 tsp. cayenne pepper

½ tsp. salt
2 C. soft shredded cheddar cheese
2 C. Rice Krispies

Mix well the flour, butter, cayenne pepper, salt and cheese. Add Rice Krispies, mix gently, but well. Roll into ½-inch balls. Place on baking sheet and flatten with a glass or palm of hand. Bake 12 mintues at 350°.

Hush Puppies

2 C. corn meal
½ C. water
1½ C. milk

2 tsp. baking powder
1 tsp. salt
1 med. onion diced

Mix all ingredients and drop by teaspoonfuls into very hot deep fat. Fry until golden brown.

Caramel Corn

2 C. brown sugar
½ C. white syrup
½ tsp. soda

2 sticks margarine (1 C.)
1 tsp. salt
8 qts. popped corn

Combine sugar, margarine, syrup and salt. Boil 5 minutes. Stir in soda after you shut off burners. Stir fast and mix soda in good. Pour corn and mix well. Put on cookie sheet and place in oven for 1 hour at 250°. Stir about every 15 minutes.

Corn Fritters

2 C. corn
2 eggs (well beaten)
½ C. milk
Flour

½ C. bacon (chopped fine)
½ tsp. salt
1 tsp. baking powder

Combine all ingredients with enough flour to make a thick batter. Drop by spoon into deep hot fat - fry to a golden brown on both sides. Drain on paper towels.

Apple Fritters

1 C. flour
1½ tsp. baking powder
½ tsp. salt
1 egg (beaten)

½ to ¾ C. milk
1 T. melted margarine
1 T. sugar
1 C. peeled and diced tart apples

Sift dry ingredients together. Combine rest of ingredients and add to the dry mixture. Use right amount of milk to make right consistency batter. Fry in deep hot fat (365-375°) til done, which will take about 5 minutes. Sprinkle with powdered sugar.

Grape Juice

1 C. purple (Concord) grapes   1 C. sugar
Boiling water

Put 1 C. grapes and 1 C. sugar in sterilized quart jar. Fill jar with boiling water and seal immediately. Let set for about 6 weeks. Makes 1 delicious grape juice.

Hard Times Coffee

Mix well 2 quarts wheat bran with 1 pint yellow corn meal. Add 3 well-beaten eggs and 1 cup best sorghum molasses. Beat well; spread on pan and put to dry in oven. Use great care by stirring often while it is browning - this is the secret of good coffee. A handful is sufficient for two persons. Sweet cream improves the flavor of the brew, but, as with store-bought coffee, this is a matter of personal taste.

Onion Rings

3 lg. onions (sliced & in rings)   ½ tsp. salt
½ C. milk   1 tsp. sugar
1½ T. melted shortening   1 well beaten egg
1 C. flour (sifted)

Combine all ingredients gradually together, - mixing well as you go to make a batter. Wash onions well and let set for a while in water. Drain, separate into rings and let dry. Dip onion rings into batter and fry in deep hot oil (365°) to a golden brown on both sides. Drain on paper towels.

Egg Nog

5 eggs
6 C. whole milk
¼ C. sugar

¼ tsp. salt
2 tsp. vanilla
Nutmeg

Beat the whites of the eggs to soft peaks. Add the yolks of the eggs and beat again. Add sugar, milk and vanilla in that order slowly and beat well. Sprinkle with nutmeg to taste. Makes about 15 servings.

Apple Pumpkin Fritters

½ C. canned pumpkin
1 egg
1 C. flour
¼ C. raisins
1½ tsp. baking powder
¼ tsp. ea.: allspice, ginger, nutmeg

3 T. milk
2 T. molasses
3 T. apple butter
2 T. shortening (melted)
1 tsp. cinnamon
Powdered sugar

Mix all dry ingredients together - add raisins. Mix pumpkin, milk, egg, shortening, apple butter and molasses; - add to dry mix. Mix well till thick and smooth; - drop by spoon into deep hot fat (350°). Fry until golden brown. Coat with powdered sugar while still warm.

Corn Fritters

12 ears sweet corn
2 eggs (beaten separate)
1 C. flour

1 tsp. baking powder
½ pt. milk
Salt and pepper

Grate the ears of corn and rub it through a sieve to rid it of hulls. Combine corn with eggs beaten separately, flour, baking powder, milk, salt and pepper to taste. Mix well and drop by spoonfuls in hot deep fat. Turn and brown on both sides, take out and drain.

SALADS

Salads

Spring Salad

1 pkg. lemon gelatin
1 C. hot water
1 small onion
1 medium cucumber

1 scant C. Miracle Whip
1 lb. carton cottage cheese
Pinch of salt

Dissolve gelatin in hot water and partially chill. Chop onion and unpeeled cucumber very fine. Mix all ingredients and add to gelatin. Chill until set.

Thousand Island Dressing

1 C. mayonnaise
½ C. catsup
1½ T. onion (minced)

2½ T. green pepper (minced)
1 pimento (minced)

Combine all ingredients, mix well, - and chill. Store in airtight jar.

French Dressing

1 C. catsup
½ C. vinegar
2 tsp. salt
1 tsp. pepper
1½ C. salad oil

2 tsp. Worcestershire sauce
3 tsp. prepared mustard
2 tsp. sugar
1 tsp. paprika

Combine catsup, vinegar, Worcestershire sauce and mustard; - mix well. Add remainder of ingredients (except salad oil) and mix in well. Add oil slowly, beating as you do. Store in refrigerator in air-tight jar. Shake before using.

24-Hour Slaw

1 head cabbage	⅔ C. sugar
1 mild onion	½ C. vinegar
2 sweet green peppers	½ C. veg oil
½ C. olives	1 tsp. prepared mustard
½ C. sugar	1 tsp. celery seed
Salt to taste	

Cut up cabbage, onion, peppers and olives; - put into blender and grate. Combine in bowl with ½ sugar; - set aside. Combine in saucepan ⅔ C. sguar, vinegar, oil, mustard, celer seed and salt. Bring to boil, - stir and cook for 8 minutes. Pour over cabbage while hot. Chill for 24 hours before serving.

Cheese Salad

1 C. mild cheese	Mayonnaise
1 C. celery (diced)	¼ tsp. salt
1 C. peas	

Chop cheese into small pieces, dice celery; - mix all ingredients together. Garnish.

Chicken Salad

5 egg yolks	5 T. vingar
½ C. butter	1 T. lemon juice
2 C. cooked chicken	1 tsp. salt
1½ C. chopped celery	1 tsp. mustard
2 T. vinegar	Red pepper
Chopped nuts	1 C. whipped cream

Boil 5 T. vinegar in double boiler, stir in egg yolks, - beat until smooth. Gradually mix in butter, - then salt, pepper and mustard. Add 2 tsp. cold vinegar, lemon juice and whipped cream, - mix well. Chop chicken fine, add celery, - and then add this to above mixture. Stir in some nuts last.

Whole Apple Salad

6 large apples
¾ C. chopped pecans
Mayonnaise
Mustard

Orange juice
1½ C. chopped celery
1½ C. chopped bananas
Salad greens

Hollow out apples, leaving a cavity to till. Discard core. Take apple cut from cavities, chop up, add celery, bananas and pecans; - mix well. Add mayonnaise and mustard to taste; - mix well. With this mix, fill cavities in apples. Chill, - then serve on salad greens.

Three Bean Salad

2 C. wax beans
2 C. red kidney beans
2 C. green beans (chopped short)
½ C. vinegar
½ C. salad oil

¾ C. sugar
1 tsp. salt
½ tsp. pepper
½ C. onion (chopped fine)
½ C. green pepper (chopped)

Drain and mix all beans. Combine all other ingredients, mix well and add to beans; - mix well. Place in refrigerator to chill overnight before serving.

Pea Salad

2 C. peas (drained)
1 C. celery (chopped)
1 T. onion (grated)
Mayonnaise

⅔ C. sweet pickles (chopped)
1 C. American cheese (chopped)
¼ tsp. salt
¼ tsp. pepper

Blend all ingredients well with just enough mayonnaise to moisten. Chill before serving.

Jello Salad
(Good Salad or Dessert)

2 C. boiling water
1 sm. pkg. orange Jello
1 sm. pkg. lemon Jello
1½ C. cold water
1 can pineapple (drained & save)
1 C. pineapple juice
2 bananas (sliced)

1½ C. mini marshmallows
1 egg (beaten)
2 T. oleo
2 T. flour
½ C. sugar
1 container Cool Whip
Sharp cheese

Dissolve orange and lemon Jello in 2 C. boiling water; add 1½ C. cold water. Blend together drained pineapple, bananas and mini marshmallows; add the Jello mixture. Place mixture into serving bowl.

TOPPING: Combine sugar, egg, oleo, flour and pineapple. Place on heat, stir and barely bring to a boil, and cool compeletly. Fold a container of Cool Whip into cooled topping mixture. Spread topping on top of first mixture; grate sharp cheese on top.

Green Spinach Salad

2 C. mayonnaise
1 C. sour cream
1 pkg. ranch style dressing
1 C. Cheddar cheese (shredded)
Salt and pepper

1 lb. bacon (fried, drained & crumbled)
6 eggs (hard boiled & sliced)
Lettuce (chopped)
5 green onions (chopped)
Green spinach (chopped)

Use a large bowl. Layer as follows: green spinach, bacon, sliced eggs, salt and pepper (to taste), lettuce and onions. In another bowl combine dressing mix and sour cream, then spread over top of salad. Sprinkle cheese over top. Chill before serving.

Homemade Salad Dressing

2 eggs (beaten)
½ C. cream
½ C. vinegar

Pinch of salt
½-¾ C. sugar

Stir together and bring to a boil over low heat, stirring constantly. Cook until thick, then cool.

Macaroni Salad

1 lb. ring macaroni
1 lg. green pepper

4 shredded carrots
1 onion (chopped)

1 can sweetened condensed milk
1 C. sugar
1 C. vinegar

2 C. mayonnaise
1 tsp. salt
¼ tsp. pepper

Cook and coll ring macaroni, then add pepper, carrots and onion.

For Dressing: Combine condensed milk, sugar, vinegar, mayonnaise, salt and pepper. Pour dressing over macaroni mixture. Chill for 4 hours. Makes large salad, it may seem soupy, but it absorbs as it sets.

Macaroni Salad

1 box shell macaroni
1 green pepper (chopped)
1 small onion (chopped)

Celery seed
Hellman's mayonnaise

Cook macaroni in salt water until tender. Drain and cool in cold water. Drain again. Mix all together with desired amount of celery seed and mayonnaise.

Cauliflower And Broccoli Salad

1 head of cauliflower
1 bunch of broccoli
1 red onion

⅓ C. sugar
⅓ C. mayonnaise
⅓ C. oil

Wash and cut into pieces the cauliflower, broccoli and onion. Mix sugar, mayonnaise and oil. Pour over vegetables and marinate overnight.

Cabbage Salad

1 head of cabbage
1 onion
1 red onion
1 green pepper

1 C. vinegar
1 C. sugar
Celery seed

Shred cabbage, onion and pepper. Salt down and let set at least 2 hours, then drain. Boil vinegar, sugar and celery seed. Cool and pour over cabbage. This will keep a long time in refrigerator.

Vegetable Salad

1 can whole kernel corn
1 can French-style green beans
1 can peas
1 C. chopped celery
1 C. chopped onion

1 C. chopped green pepper
¾ C. vinegar
1 C. sugar
1 tsp. salt
1 T. water

Drain corn, beans and peas. Mix with remaining vegetables. Boil vinegar, sugar, salt and water. Let cool and pour over vegetables. Let stand overnight. Will keep at least 2 weeks in refrigerator.

Macaroni Salad

1 pt. mayonnaise
1 C. vineger
1½ C. sugar
1 can Eagle Brand milk

1 lb. twist macaroni
1 green pepper (chopped)
2 grated carrots
1 chopped onion

Cook macaroni according to directions on package; drain. Stir mayonnaise, vinegar, sugar and milk until smooth. Fold in macaroni and vegetables. Cover tightly and refrigerate for 3-4 hours or overnight.

Shell Macaroni Salad

1 lb. shell macaroni
4 carrots (grated)
4 stalks celery (chopped)
1 small onion (chopped)
10 radishes (sliced)

¾ C. vinegar
1 C. sugar
2 C. real mayonnaise
1 can Eagle Brand milk
1 tsp. salt
½ tsp. pepper

Cook macaroni until done. Drain and rinse with cold water, mix with chopped vegetables. Heat vinegar and sugar until sugar is dissolved. Cool, then add mayonnaise, Eagle Brand milk, salt and pepper. Beat until smooth and creamy. Pour over macaroni and vegetables and mix. Better if made day before.

Broccoli And Cauliflower Salad

2 C. chopped broccoli
2 C. chopped cauliflower
1 C. chopped pepper (half red)
1 C. chopped celery
1 C. chopped & seeded tomatoes
1 C. cubed cheese (cheddar)

6 green onions (chopped)
1 C. mayonnaise
1 C. sour cream
1 T. lemon juice
1 T. powdered sugar

Combine broccoli, cauliflower, peppers, celery, tomatoes, cheese and onions. Blend together mayonnaise, sour cream, lemon juice and powdered sugar. Pour over vegetables and toss until well coated. This makes a large salad and will serve 15-20 people.

Bean Salad

3½ C. dried beans (cooked)
1 C. chopped tomato
⅓ C. sweet pickles (chopped)
¼ tsp. vinegar
¼ C. salad oil
Salad greens

3 T. onion (minced)
1 tsp. sugar
½ tsp. paprika
1 tsp. salt
Chopped spinach

Make a bean mix with beans, tomatoes, pickles, celery and onion. In another bowl, place over ingredients, blend in well. Pour this mix over bean mix. Serve on salad greens.

Potato Salad

6 lg. potatoes (boiled & cooked)
4 hard boiled eggs (cooled)
1 small onion

Salt and pepper
Salad dressing

Dice or better yet, slice potatoes and then take a sharp knife and slice through several times until cut as desired. Cube eggs and onion; add to potatoes. Salt and pepper, to suit taste. You can add a dash of celery seed too. Now for the dressing, use a blend of ½ Miracle Whip, ½ homemade dressing or if in a hurry take the Miracle Whip and stir in some sugar and cream (milk or Half and Half may be used) until you have the right consistency and taste (you will have to sample it).

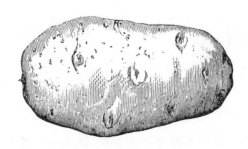

Hot Slaw

Shread one small heat of cabbage, put in a saucepan with 2 T. water. Cook until tender, stirring frequently, then drain. Make a dressing of these ingredients:

2 eggs (well beaten)	*1 T. butter*
⅓ C. vinegar	*2 T. sugar*
⅔ C. milk	*Salt and pepper to taste*

Beat ingredients together, turn over cooked cabbage and cook until dressing thickens.

Three Bean Salad

1 can green beans	*¾ C. sugar*
1 can yellow wax beans	*½ C. oil*
1 can red kidney beans	*½ C. vinegar*
1 green pepper (chopped)	*1 tsp. salt*
1 medium onion (chopped)	*1 tsp. pepper*
¾ C. celery (chopped)	

Drain beans and add remaining vegetables. Combine sugar, oil, vinegar, salt and pepper; pour over the beans. Let stand overnight.

SOUPS

Soups

Winter Soup

1½ lbs. beef chunks	2 C. cabbage (shredded)
1 onion (quartered)	2 T. veg oil
1 T. salt	1 onion (sliced)
¼ tsp. pepper	1 garlic clove (minced)
2 qts. water	1 T. parsley (chopped)
2 stalks celery (chopped)	¼ tsp. oregano
2 C. canned tomatoes (chopped)	¼ C. Parmesan cheese (grated)
2 C. carrots (chopped)	½ C. small egg noodles
2 C. kidney beans	

Place meat, quartered onion, 2 qts. water, salt and pepper in stew pan. Bring to a boil and let simmer for 2 hours. Remove meat,, strain stock. Add enough water to stock to make 2½ qts. In skillet heat oil to hot and stirring, saute celery, sliced onion, garlic and parsley for 10 minutes. Dice meat and add to stock in stew pot. Add tomatoes, carrots, cabbage and sauted contents of skillet. Place cover on and let simmer for 1¼ hours. Stir in beans, oregano and noodles, let cook for 15 minutes or longer until noodles are tender. Stir in cheese and serve.

Chicken Gumbo Soup

1 chicken	6 med. tomatoes (sliced)
½ C. salt pork fat	3 C. boiling water
1 lg. onion (sliced thin)	2 T. salt
4 C. okra (chopped fine)	3 parsley springs (chopped)
1 C. cream	¼ tsp. cayenne
1 C. boiled rice	

Cut chicken into small pieces, saute in pork fat. Remove chicken and place in stewpan. Saute onions in same fat for 10 minutes. Add tomatoes, parsley and okra; saute for another 30 minutes. Combine with chicken; add boiling water and seasonings. Let simmer until chicken is very tender (3-4 hours). Add cream and rice and more seasoning if needed. Bring to a good boil, then serve.

Potato Soup

Use one dozen potatoes. Peel thinly, sliced; and boil till tender to a fork. Add finely-slivered celery tops, parsley and onion (to taste) to the drained potatoes. Add 2 qts. sweet milk and bring to a boil. Season to taste with freshly ground pepper and some salt.

Hamburger Soup

1 lb. hamburger	1 C. diced potatoes
2 tsp. salt	¼ C. rice
¼ tsp. pepper	5 C. water
1 C. diced carrots	2 C. tomato juice
½ C. diced onion	

Brown hamburger and drain. Mix hamburger with remaining ingredients. Simmer 1 hour.

Southern Corn Pone

Mix with cold water into a soft dough one quart of southern corn meal (sifted), 1 tsp. salt 1 T. butter or melted lard. Mold into oval cakes with the hands and bake in a very hot oven, in well greased pans. To be eaten hot. The crust should be brown.

Potato Soup

6-8 lg. potatoes
1 lg. onion
4 stalks celery
¼ lb. oleo

1 C. cold milk
1 egg and 1 C. cold milk
   (beaten together)

Cut up and cook vegetables until well done. Add oleo. Mash with potato masher and add 1 C. cold milk. Stir and add egg and milk mixture. Heat until hot but do not boil. Add salt and pepper to taste.

Asparagus Soup

1 qt. asparagus (chopped in 1-inch
   pieces)
1 qt. water
2 C. milk

1 T. flour
1 T. butter
Salt and pepper
Toasted bread (diced)

Using 1 qt. water, boil asparagus until tender. Rub asparagus through colander back into water in which it was cooked. Heat milk; add flour and butter and let cook a little. Add seasonings and then add the asparagus. Let boil for 10 minutes, then pour over toasted and diced bread.

Bean Soup

1¼ lbs. navy beans
3½ C. chopped onions
2¾ C. chopped celery
1 ham bone

¼ C. chopped parsley
2 tsp. salt
1 tsp. black pepper
¾ C. mashed potatoes

Soak beans overnight. Combine beans and ham bone with enough water to cover. Bring to boil and let simmer for about 1 hour or longer. Add remainder of ingredients, bring to a boil, and simmer till beans are tender. Remove bone but chop meat off to go back into soup.

Catfish Soup

2-3 lbs. catfish (cut up)
2 qts. cold water
1 sliced onion
1 chopped celery stalk

Salt and pepper
Herbs (bay leaf, parsley, thyme)
1 C. milk
2 T. butter or fat

Place all ingredients into stew pan and put on slow fire. Stir occasionally and cook until fish is ready to fall to pieces. Serve hot.

Cheese-Potato Soup

1 carrot (sliced)
1 onion (sliced)
4 potatoes (chopped)
2 C. Velveeta cheese (chopped)
3 chicken bouillon cubes

1 stick oleo
3 T. flour
3 C. milk
Salt and pepper (to taste)

Combine vegetables and bouillon cubes with enough water to cover. Bring to a boil and cook until tender. In a saucepan cook milk, flour and oleo until thickened, then stir in cheese. Stir and cook until cheese is melted, then add to vegetables. Season to taste, heat almost to a boil and serve.

Vegetable Beef Barley Soup

3 T. salad oil
2 lbs. beef chunk (cut into ¾-inch cubes; I use stew meat)
2 C. chopped onions
1 tsp. minced garlic
½ tsp. thyme
½ tsp. marjoram
6 C. water

2 cans (about 14 oz. ea.) beef broth
1½ C. diced carrots
¾ C. diced celery
1½ tsp. salt
½ tsp. freshly ground pepper
3 C. diced potatoes
¾ C. barley

In large pot, heat oil over medium high heat. Add meat and cook, stirring occasionally, until browned on all sides. Add onions, garlic, thyme and marjoram. Cook, stirring 10 minutes more. Add water, beef broth, carrots, celery, barley*, salt and pepper. Bring to a boil; reduce heat and simmer uncovered 1½ hours. Add potatoes. Bring to a boil; reduce heat and simmer uncovered 30-40 minutes, until potatoes are tender. (*If using quick barley, add with the potatoes.) Makes 14 C., 225 calories per cup.

Easy Broccoli Cheese Soup

1 (16 oz.) pkg. frozen chopped broccoli
2 T. butter or margarine
Diced ham (opt.)

1 medium onion (diced)
Milk
3 cans chedder cheese soup

Cook onions with broccoli according to package directions on broccoli. Drain excess water if any. Add butter or margarine. Mix well the cheese soup and using the soup can to measure, add 2½-3 cans milk. Add soup to broccoli and heat well. Add diced ham if desired.

Easy Cheddar Chowder

2 C. boiling water
2 C. chopped potatoes
½ C. carrot slices
¼ C. chopped onion
½ C. celery slices
1½ tsp. salt
1 C. ham cubes

¼ tsp. pepper
¼ C. margarine
¼ C. flour
2 C. milk
2 C. shredded sharp natural
   cheese

Combine water, vegetables and seasonings. Cover; simmer 10 minutes. Do not drain. Make a white sauce with margarine, flour and milk. Add cheese. Stir until melted. Add ham and undrained vegetables. Heat. Do not boil. Makes 6-8 servings.

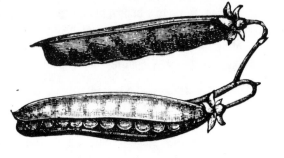

Beef Stew

⅔ C. flour
1½ tsp. salt
½ tsp. pepper
3 lbs. boneless stew beef
  (cut in 1-inch cubes)
4 T. fat or oil
6 C. water

6 medium-size onions (sliced)
8 medium-size potatoes (cut in
  1-inch cubes)
10 medium-size carrots (quartered)
3 C. frozen peas (if desired)
4 stalks celery (cut up)
¼ C. water

Combine flour, salt and pepper. Coat meat with seasoned flour. Save remaining flour. Brown meat in hot fat in a 4-qt. saucepan. Add water and cover tightly. Simmer until meat is tender, about 1½ hours. Add onions, potatoes, celery and carrots. Cover and simmer until all vegetables are tender. Blend ¼ C. water with remaining flour. Add to stew, stirring gently. Cook until thick. Serves 12.

Vegetable Beef Soup

2 T. vegetable oil
1 lb. boneless beef chuck
  (1-inch cubes)
1 C. onion
3 T. flour
1 (14 oz.) can beef broth

1 (16 oz.) can whole tomatoes
½ tsp. celery salt
1½ C. uncooked macaroni
1 C. frozen peas
1 C. frozen corn

Heat oil over hight heat in 5 qt. saucepan. Add meat and brown on all sides about 5 minutes. Reduce heat to moderate; add onions and cook 5-7 minutes, stirring several times, until soft. Stir in flour. Whisk in beef broth and gently scrape bottom of pot to loosen brown particles. Stir in tomatoes, celery salt and 3 C. water. Bring to a boil, reduce heat, cover and simmer 45 minutes. Add macaroni, corn and peas. Increase heat to moderate, cover and boil 20 minutes, stirring occasionally to keep pasta from sticking. Makes 8 C. at 282 calories each.

Ribbles For Soup

1 egg
Dash of salt

2 C. flour

Ribbles are thin strands of dough used to thicken soups. They may be as thick or as fine as you like. To make: Beat the egg and work the flour into egg by rubbing the mixture with the fingers to desired thinness. Add ribbles to soup 10 minutes before serving and simmer.

"Just For Notes"

MAIN

DISHES

Main Dishes

Main Dishes - Continued

Main Dishes - Continued

Pork Chops Wow!

8 pork chops
2 tsp. salt
½ tsp. pepper
8 thin onion slices

8 green pepper rings
8 T. uncooked instant rice
1 (16 oz.) can stewed tomatoes

In large skillet brown chops over medium heat. Sprinkle with salt and pepper. Top each with 1 onion slice, 1 green pepper ring, 1 T. rice, ¼ C. tomatoes. Reduce heat, cover and simmer until done, about 45 minutes. Add small amount of water if necessary.

Meat Stew

1½ lbs. boneless beef stew meat
1 tsp. salt
½ tsp. paprika
¼ C. flour
2 T. fat

2 C. water
3 T. catsup
6 medium potatoes (peeled)
6 medium carrots (peeled)
4 medium onions

Cut meat into small pieces, roll in seasoned flour and brown in the fat in a heavy kettle. Make sure every piece is well browned for best flavor. Add 2 C. water and simmer in tightly covered kettle till meat is tender (about 2 hours). Then add vegetables which have been cut into fairly large chunks and continue cooking in covered kettle until vegetables are tender. Add 3 T. catsup, salt, to taste and just a little flour to thicken if broth is too soupy. (Mix flour in cold water before adding.) Serve while steaming hot.

Beef Red (Corned)

Cut up a quarter of beef. For each 100 lbs. of beef, use ½ peek of coarse salt, ¼ lb. salt-petre, ¼ lb. saleratus and 1 qt. sorghum molasses (or 2 lb. brown sugar). Scatter some salt in the bottom of a pickle tub or barrel. Add a layer of meat. Alternate salt and meat till all is used. Let remain overnight. Dissolve saleratus and salt-petre in a little warm water with molasses; pour over meat to cover. Weigh down meat so it will stay under brine. It is fit to use after 10 days. Use a little more salt in hot weather.

Use-It-Up Beef Balls

1 lb. left-over beef (roast or steak)
2 C. fine rolled crackers or grated
  bread crumbs
Lemon and onion

Milk (or gravy)
2 eggs
Butter
Salt and pepper

Take the cold left-over beef, cut off all gristle or bone and hash it fine. Combine with the crackers (or bread crumbs), milk (or gravy) to moisten, eggs. Season to taste with butter, salt and pepper; lemon and onion if you like. Let stand till it swells and then make into patties or rolls. Brown in deep fat consisting of ½ batter.

Snappin' Turtle

Success of preparing turtle to eat depends a great deal on proper dressing. To dress an snapping turtle, scrub all mud and dirt from him and then cut off head and toes. With a spike nail, secure turtle to a large plank or slab, breast up, by piercing center of the breast bone. With a sharp knife cut skin loose from shell around one front leg, then the other, separating in two pieces at the neck. Then pull the skin off one leg, then the other. This can be done more easily with two persons working together, one at each end pulling against each other. Start with the right front leg and left hind leg, then grasp both legs and neck in one hand and insert the point of a stout knife at base of neck bone and giving a twist until the legs and neck come loose. Use same procedure on hind legs and tail. Remove breast bone, spike and entrails. Then with a sharp hatchet or clever chop along tenderloin on each side,then trim top shell loose. Trim all of water fat from meat and discard. Rinse and meat is ready to use in any of following recipes.

Fried Turtle

To fry turtle it is advised to parboil or cook in pressure cooker until tender first. Then roll in flour or meal and seasonings. Fry in deep fat.

Sweet And Sour Pork

1½ lbs. pork (cut in chunks)
1 T. oil
1 bell pepper (chunked)

1 onion (chopped)
2 carrots (sliced)
1 lg. can pineapple chunks with
   juice

SAUCE:
1 C. catsup
⅓ C. brown sugar
2 T. lemon juice

1 T. soy sauce
1 tsp. ginger (ground)

Brown meat in oil. Mix sauce and remaining ingredients with meat and simmer over low heat for 20 minutes. Serve over rice. (If preferred, chicken can be substituted for the pork.)

Glorified Hamburgers

1 lb. hamburger
12 soda crackers (broken up)
Salt and pepper to taste

1 egg (beaten)
¾ C. milk

GRAVY:
1 C. diced onions
⅓ C. flour

3 C. water
Salt and pepper

Mix hamburger, crackers, egg and milk together and form into 6 thick patties. Brown slowly until partially done and put in roaster and set aside and make the gravy. Simmer the onions in the skillet in which patties were browned, until they are slightly browned. Then add the flour, stirring well. Add the water and cook. Pour over patties and simmer at 300° for 1 hour or longer.

Barbecued Meat Balls

MEAT BALLS:

1½ lbs. ground beef
1 C. crackers
½ C. milk
1 tsp. garlic salt

2 beaten eggs
Small onion (diced)
Salt and pepper

SAUCE:

1 C. ketchup
½ C. tomato juice or soup
1 C. water
4 T. brown sugar

1 tsp. celery salt
1 T. vinegar
½ tsp. salt
1 T. hot sauce

Mix all meatball ingredients together and roll into balls. Brown on both sides, drain. Pour sauce over meat balls. Simmer 45-50 minutes.

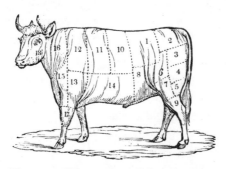

Easy Cheesy Meat Loaf

1½ lbs. lean ground beef
2 C. fresh bread crumbs (4 slices bread)
1 C. tomato juice
⅓ C. chopped onion

2 eggs
2 tsp. beef flavor instant bouillon
¼ tsp. pepper
6 slices American cheese

Preheat oven to 350°. In large bowl combine all ingredients except cheese. Mix well. In shallow baking dish, shape half the mixture into loaf. Cut 4 slices cheese into strips. Arrange on meat. Top with remaining meat. Press edges together to seal. Bake 1 hour. Pour off fat. Top with remaining cheese slices. Refrigerate leftovers.

Meat Loaf

1½ lbs. ground beef
¼ C. chopped onion
¾ C. oatmeal
1½ tsp. salt

½ C. catsup
¼ tsp. pepper
½ C. milk
1 beaten egg

Preheat oven to 350°. Thoroughly mix together milk, catsup, beaten egg, salt and pepper. Combine with ground beef, onion and oatmeal. Press into ungreased loaf pan and bake approximately 60-65 minutes; or divide into two small loaf pans, bake one 30-35 minutes and freeze the other one for later use. (Thaw before baking.) Drain. Let stand before slicing.

Pork Chops

4 pork chops
2 T. butter
1 onion (chopped)

2 apples (peeled, cored and sliced)
and/or sweet potatoes
1½ C. apple juice

Melt butter in large skillet. Brown pork chops for 2 minutes on both sides. Remove and put on plate. Saute onions. Put pork chops and apples back into skillet and pour apple juice over them. Cover, reduce heat and simmer for 1 hour. Relax and enjoy the aroma.

Fried Rabbit

1 C. flour
1 tsp. salt
Pepper to taste

Cooking fat
1 diced onion
Juice of ¼ lemon

Cut rabbit up in pieces desired. Roll pieces in mixture of flour, salt and pepper. Brown the rabbit in ast least 4 T. cooking fat an then add diced onions and lemon juice. Cover and cook until done.

Wrapped-Up Pups

2 C. buttermilk baking mix
½ C. undiluted Carnation evaporated
  milk

½ C. chopped onion
¼ C. prepared mustard
1 lb. (10) weiners

Combine baking mix, Carnation milk and mustard. Stir with fork until soft dough forms. Add onion; mix until blended. On lightly floured board, knead dough about 5 times. Divide dough into 10 parts and roll into balls. Flatten dough to ¼-inch thickness, using palm of hands. Wrap weiners in dough. Roll weiners on board until dough seams are sealed. Place on cookie sheet. Bake in very hot oven (450°) for 14 minutes.

Rabbit Pie

2 rabbits (cut into suitable pieces)
⅔ C. water
½ lb. salt pork (chopped)
½ C. butter
6 boiled potatoes (chopped)
Pie crust pastry

1 onion (chopped)
3 cloves
6 olives (chopped)
Salt
Pepper
3 T. parsley (minced)
Browned flour

Line a baking dish with pie crust dough and have enough dough to cover top. Combine rabbit, water, pork, onion, cloves, olives, slat and pepper (to taste) in a stew pot. Boil until tender, adding a little water if necessary. Using browned flour, thicken, let it boil, then add butter. Remove from heat. In pastry lined dish, alternate layers of stew with potatoes until all is in, then top with pastry crust. Cut slits in top; bake until crust is done.

Broccoli-Cauliflower Casserole

1 head of raw cauliflower
1 bunch of raw broccoli
1 can cream of mushroom soup

1 C. Minute Rice
1 large jar Cheez Whiz
½ C. milk

Break cauliflower and broccoli into flowerettes and boil til tender. Drain and put in a large casserole dish. Cook Minute Rice as directed and add to vegetables. Melt Cheez Whiz and spread over rice and vegetables. Mix milk and soup; add. Bake at 350° for 1 hour.

Broccoli, Ham And Cheese Casserole

2 C. cooked ham (diced)
2 C. cooked noodles
1 pkg. frozen broccoli (cooked)
1 can cream of celery soup

½ C. Cheddar cheese (grated)
½ C. mozzarella cheese (grated)
Cheese crackers

Make a cheese sauce by melting Cheddar cheese and cream of celery soup together. Combine ham, cooked and drained broccoli and cheese sauce. Layer alternately in 9×13-inch casserole, noodles sauce, noodles, sauce. Top with mozzarella cheese and crumbled crackers. Bake at 350° for 30 minutes.

Meat Balls

1 lb. ground beef
½ C. homemade bread crumbs
1 T. minced onion
½ tsp. horseradish

2 drops hot pepper sauce
2 eggs (beaten)
¼ tsp. salt
¼ tsp. pepper

SAUCE:
¾ C. catsup
½ C. water
¼ C. cider vinegar
3 T. brown sugar
1½ tsp. crushed onion
Cayenne pepper to taste

2 tsp. Worcestershire sauce
½ tsp. salt
1 tsp. mustard
¼ tsp. pepper
3 drops hot pepper sauce

Heat broiler. Mix all meat ingredients and shape into meat balls about ½-inch to ¾-inch in size. Brown on all sides; drain fat. Combine ingredients for sauce in large Dutch oven and put meat balls into sauce. Simmer about 30 minutes or more. Makes about 3 dozen balls. (NOTE: Flavor improves if made a day ahead.)

Barbecued Brisket

4 lbs. beef brisket

Sprinkle meat with white garlic salt, celery salt, onion salt and pepper and ½ bottle liquid smoke. Marinate overnight. Bake at 275° in covered Pyrex for 4 hours.

SAUCE:
¾ C. brown sugar
½ C. catsup
Dash of nutmeg

1 tsp. mustard
1 C. barbecue sauce
Dash of Worcestershire sauce

Mix ingredients and heat. Remove meat from oven and brush with ½ of mixture. Cook ½ hour longer. Then slice and brush with rest of sauce or just put on table.

Corned Beef Casserole

1 (16 oz.) pkg. elbow macaroni
1 (12 oz.) can corned beef
¼ lb. American cheese (cubed)
1 can cream of chicken soup

1 C. milk (or more)
½ C. chopped onions
¾ C. buttered bread crumbs
Salt and pepper to taste

Cook macaroni, drain. Mix all ingredients together, except bread crumbs, putting them over the top. Bake in a 325° oven about 1½ hours.

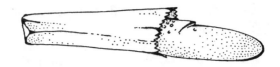

Goulash

1 small box macaroni
1 lb. hamburger
1 onion

1 sm. can tomato sauce or whole
tomatoes

Cook macaroni as directed on box. Brown hamburger and onion until done. Add tomatoes or sauce. Bring to a boil for a few minutes. Salt and pepper to taste.

Cabbage Casserole

1 sm. head cabbage
1 sm. onion (diced)
1 lb. hamburger

¼ C. rice (uncooked)
1 can condensed tomato soup
1 C. water

Cut cabbage into quarters. Place in bottom of large casserole dish. Mix soup and water. Add remaining ingredients. Season to taste. Bake at 350° for 1 hour.

Chicken Stew

3 lbs. chicken parts	*½ C. sliced*
2 C. diced onions	*2 bay leaves*
2 C. diced celery	*½ tsp. ground thyme*
2 C. red or green bell peppers	*½ tsp. basil leaves*
4 C. canned tomatoes with liquid	*½ tsp. chili powder*
½ C. fresh or frozen green beans	*½ tsp. each salt and pepper*
	if desired

Skin the chicken parts and set aside. Discard skin. In a crock pot or slow cooker combine all other ingredients. Stir to combine. Place chicken parts on top. Cover and let cook 8-10 hours on low or 5-6 hours on high. Remove chicken parts and allow to cool slightly. Remove bones, cut into pieces and return to pot for 30 minutes. Remove bay leaves before serving. Makes 4 large servings. Each serving provides 4 protein exchanges and $5\frac{2}{3}$ vegetable exchanges.

Dumplings

¾ C. sifted flour	*1 egg*
½ C. milk	*2 tsp. baking powder*
½ tsp. salt	

Sift the flour, baking powder and salt together. Beat egg; add milk. Then mix all ingredients together just enough to moisten the flour. Drop batter by spoon into boiling gravy. Cover tightly to hold in the steam and boil gently for 15 minutes without opening the pot. Serve at once with meat and gravy.

Barbecued Chicken Special

3 broilers (cut in pieces or
   quartered)
½ tsp. salt
¼ C. oil

½ C. lemon juice
2 T. chopped onion
½ tsp. black pepper
¼ tsp. paprika

Wash and wipe chicken. Mix remaining ingredients. Brush sauce on both sides of chicken and let stand 30-60 minutes. Place chicken on grill and brush with sauce. Turn chicken occasionally so it browns evenly. Cook about 1 hour or until done. Serves 6-8.

Fish Chowder
(Northern or Sheephead)

1 C. carrots
2 C. potatoes
½ C. onion

1 C. celery
2-3 lbs. fillet fish

Boil cut up fish pieces until done; strain. Save fish water for broth. In broth boil diced carrots, potatoes, onion and celery. Add salt, pepper, allspice, bay leaf and chicken broth or bouillon. Add medium white sauce.

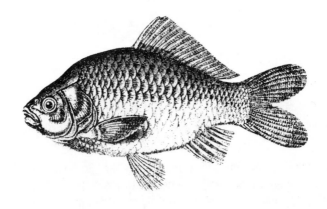

Beef Stew

2 lbs. beef stew meat or roast
  (cut into 1-inch cubes)
4 medium onions (sliced)
¼ C. soy sauce
¾ tsp. salt
½ tsp. pepper

4-6 large diced potatoes
4 large carrots (cut into chunks)
1 celery (opt.)
3 T. flour
water

Put sliced onions and meat in bottom of small roaster. Pour enough water over this to cover well. Add soy sauce. Mix flour, salt and pepper together. Pour over water and mix well. May be lumpy but these will cook out. Bake covered for 1 hour at 350°. Add carrots and celery. Bake for another ½ hour, then add potatoes. Bake for another hour or until done. Add more water if necessary, if more water is added, add some additional flour to keep broth thick. Makes 6-8 servings.

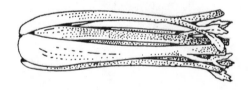

Fried Green Tomatoes

BATTER:
1 C. cornmeal
½ C. flour
2 tsp. baking powder
1 tsp. salt (or less)

1 T. sugar
Pinch of pepper
1 C. milk

6-8 green tomatoes

To Fry: Cut tomatoes into ¼-inch slices. Dip in batter and fry in deep fat, drain and serve.

Carrot Casserole

4½ C. carrots
1 stick butter
½ lb. American cheese

1 onion (chopped)
1½ C. corn flakes

Parboil carrots until tender. Melt butter and grate cheese. Layer portions, cheese, butter, carrots in a casserole and repeat with corn flakes on top. Bake at 325° for about 1 hour until cheese melts.

Sweet And Sour Sauerkraut

1 (No. 2½) can sauerkraut (drained)
1 large or 2 medium fresh tomatoes
  (sliced)
1 C. light brown packed brown sugar

1 small onion (chopped)
4 sliced bacon (fried and crumbled)
4 T. bacon grease

Toss together all ingredients and bake at 350° for 1 hour.

Cheese Scalloped Carrots

12 sliced carrots
1 minced onion
¼ C. butter or margarine
¼ C. flour
1 tsp. salt
¼ tsp. dry mustard

2 C. milk
1/8 tsp. pepper
¼ tsp. celery salt
½ lb. sharp cheese (grated)
3 C. buttered soft bread crumbs

Cook carrots until barely tender. Cook onion in butter or margarine. Slowly add flour, salt and mustard; then milk, pepper and celery salt. In a 2-qt. casserole arrange a layer of carrots, then a layer of cheese, repeat ending with a layer of carrots. Pour on sauce, top with crumbs. Bake at 350° for 35-40 minutes. Serves 8.

Scalloped Cabbage

Cabbage
Salt, pepper
Flour

Grated American cheese
Milk

Layer grated cabbage into casserole in layers. Sprinkle flour, salt, pepper and grated American cheese over each layer. Barely cover with milk or Half and Half. Put cracker crumbs on top. Bake 1 hour at 350° or until done.

Sweet Potato

1 butternut squash
1 C. brown sugar
¼ C. water

¼ C. butter
½ tsp. salt

Pare squash and cut into chunks. Place in buttered casserole. Make syrup of brown sugar, water, butter and salt. Pour over squash. Cover lightly with aluminum foil. Bake at 325° approximately 1 hour, basting occasionally. Uncover last half of baking time.

Vegetable Chowder

2 C. diced potatoes
¾ C. diced onions
½ C. diced celery
½ C. diced carrots
2½ C. boiling water
2 tsp. salt
4 T. flour
4 T. oleo (melted)

2 C. milk
½ tsp. pepper
½ tsp. dried mustard
½ T. minced parsley
¼ lb. grated cheddar cheese
1 C. canned tomatoes with pinch
    soda in them
¼ C. sugar (to suit taste)
1 can creamed corn

Put potatoes, onions, celery and carrots in boiling water with salt. Cook until tender. In saucepan mix flour and oleo together. Add milk and mix well. Add pepper, mustard, parsley and cheese. Pour cooked vegetables and sauce together. Add tomatoes, sugar and creamed corn. Heat well and serve. Freeze well.

Sauerkraut Casserole

5 strips bacon (fried and crumbled) *2 lbs. sauerkraut*
1 sm. onion (chopped) *1 can tomatoes (drained)*
1 C. brown sugar

Combine and bake 1 hour at 350°.

Corn Casserole

1 beaten egg *Salt and pepper to taste*
⅔ C. milk *¼ C. chopped onion*
1 can cream style corn *¼ C. chopped green pepper*
1 can whole corn *1 small jar pimentos*
1 stick melted margarine *1 C. cracker crumbs*
2 T. sugar *1 C. grated cheese*

Mix in order given. Bake in greased casserole 1 hour at 350°.

Spaghetti Pie

6 oz. spaghetti
⅓ C. grated Parmesan cheese
1 C. cottage cheese (8 oz.)
½ C. chopped onion
1 (8 oz.) can (1 C.) tomatoes
  (cut up)
1 tsp. sugar
½ tsp. garlic salt
2 T. butter or margarine

2 well beaten eggs
1 lb. ground beef or bulk pork
  sausage
¼ C. chopped green pepper
1 (6 oz.) can tomato paste
1 tsp. dried oregano (crushed)
½ C. shredded mozzarella cheese
  (2 oz.)

Cook the spaghetti according to package directions; drain. (Should have about 3 C. spaghetti.) Stir butter or margarine into hot spaghetti. Stir in Parmesan cheese and eggs. Form spaghetti mixture into a "crust" in a buttered 10-inch pie plate. Spread cottage cheese over botom of spaghetti crust. In skillet cook ground beef or pork sausage, onion and green pepper until vegetables are tender and meat is browned. Drain off excess fat. Stir in undrained tomatoes, tomato paste, sugar, oregano and garlic satl; heat through. Turn meat mixture into spaghetti crust. Bake, uncovered, in 350° oven for 20 minutes. Sprinkle the mozzarella cheese atop. Bake 5 minutes longer or until cheese melts. Makes 6 servings.

Fannies Corn Fritters

1 C. canned corn
1 egg (well beaten)
⅔ C. flour

2¾ tsp. baking powder
1 tsp. salt
Few grains of pepper

Mix ingredients in order. Drop by spoonfuls in deep fat. Fry until golden brown.

Scalloped Potatoes

4½ C. thinly sliced potatoes
½ C. thinly sliced Velveeta cheese
¼ C. thinly chopped onions
2 tsp. salt
1/8 tsp. pepper

5 T. margarine or butter
5 T. flour
1¼ tsp. salt
Dash of pepper
2½ C. milk

Melt margarine, add flour, 1¼ tsp. salt and dash of pepper. Stir until smooth. Add milk slowly, stirring constantly. Cook over medium heat until smooth and thickened, stirring constantly. Put ⅓ of potatoes onions and cheese in 2 qt. baking dish. Salt and pepper this. Pour ⅓ of sauce over this. Repeat until potatoes, cheese, onions and sauce are gone - ending with sauce. Bake at 350° for ¾-1 hour, covered. Uncovered and bake for an additional ¼-½ hour.

Crunch Top Potatoes

6 T. butter or margarine
3 or 4 large baking potatoes (pared
    and cut in ½-inch crosswise
    slices)

¾ C. crushed cornflakes
1 tsp. paprika
1 tsp. salt

Melt butter in 15½ x 10½-inch pan; like flat cookie or jelly roll pan. Add single layer or sliced potatoes, turn once in the melted fat or butter. Mix the crushed cornflakes, cheese, salt and paprika. Sprinkle over the top. Bake at 350° for ½ hour or until done and tops are crisp.

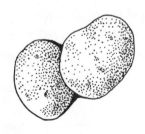

Scalloped Corn Supreme

1 (1 lb.) can (2 C.) golden cream
  style corn
1 C. milk
1 well beaten egg
1 C. cracker crumbs

¼ C. minced onion
3 T. chopped pimento
¾ tsp. salt
½ C. buttered cracker crumbs

Heat corn and milk. Gradually stir in egg. And next 4 ingredients and dash of pepper. Mix well. Pour into greased 8-inch round baking dish. Sprinkle butter crumbs over top. Bake at 350° for 20 minutes. Serves 6.

Creamed Tomatoes

MIX TOGETHER IN PAN:
¼ lb. oleo
¼ C. sugar

¼ C. flour

Add to mixture above 1 quart of tomatoes, heat until boiling. Add 1 C. cooked macaroni.

Beer Batter

Pancake mix
Salt

Beer

This is a simple recipe. Use a good pancake mix, add enough beer to make a rather medium thin batter. Add salt to taste (the batter will have to taste salty if you do not salt the fish or whatever you wish to cook.) Dip fillets in this batter and fry in deep hot fat (340°). Drain on paper towels.

Fish Fritters

1 lb. fish fillets
3 eggs (separated)
3 T. flour

Minced garlic
Minced parsley
Salt and pepper

Boil fish, drain, and mash. Beat egg yolks until light and thicker. Add flour slowly; then garlic, parsley, salt and pepper (to taste), mix well as you add. Stir in fish. Beat egg whites to froth and blend in. Drop by spoon in deep hot oil (365°). Fry to a golden brown on both sides. Drain on paper towels.

Spanish Rice

¼ C. vegetable oil
¼ C. minced onions
¼ C. chopped celery
1½ C. rice
1 (No. 2) can tomatoes
⅔ C. tomato catsup
2 C. hot water

2 C. hot water
2 tsp. salt
1 lb. ground beef
¾ C. choppeed green pepper
11 oz. beef bouillon
1 tsp. sugar
Tomato juice

Heat oil in skillet, and brown onions and celery. Combine rice, tomatoes, tomato catsup, hot water and salt; mix well and add to skillet. Cover bring to boil and let simmer for 10 minutes. In another skillet, brown ground beef and pepper, then add bouillon and sugar. Add this mix to above mix, then pour into 3 qt. baking dish. Bake in moderate oven (350°) for 35 minutes. Add some tomato juice if necessary; stir occasionally. Serve 8-10.

Rabbit Or Squirrel Stew

Rabbit (or squirrel)
1 qt. water
3-4 slices bacon
3 potatoes (chopped)
1 small can tomatoes

2 beef bouillon cubes
1 C. whole grain corn
1 large onion (chopped)
Salt and pepper

Place water in a stew pan, along with cut up rabbit (or squirrel). Cut up bacon and add. Let simmer until meat is tender, then all remainder of ingredients. Salt and pepper well. Let stew until potatoes are tender, then serve. Good with corn bread.

Fried Pies

4 C. flour
2 eggs
6 T. margarine
1 C. milk
Fruit (apples, peaches)

2 tsp. baking powder
1 tsp. salt
1 tsp. cinnamon
1 tsp. ground nutmeg
3 T. sugar

Sift flour; add baking powder, salt and butter; mix well together. Beat egg and milk; add this mix slowly to the flour mix. Mix until stiff dough, then roll out thin, and cut into 5-6-inch circles. Peel and cut apples (peaches) into sliced and place equally on dough circles. Combine sugar, cinnamon and nutmeg in cup, sprinkle this mix over fruit. Fold dough over, seal edges with fork dipped in milk. Fry in deep hot fat (about 375°) till golden brown. Let cool on paper towels.

Ground Hog

When ground hog is dressed be sure to remove the kernel from under the front legs to keep from making it taste. Cut up and salt to taste. Roll in flour, put in hot fat and fry until brown. Then put in inset pans in pressure cooker with ½ lbs. pressure. Possum cna be cooked the same way with good results.

Coon And Dressing

Cook coon into small pieces and salt to taste. Cook in the inset pan of the pressure cooker for about an hour at 15 lb. pressure. Cook longer if it is an old and tough coon. When coon is tender, arrange pieces in a baking dish and cover with dressing made as follows: Moisten 8-10 slices of dry bread with the juice cooked from the coon and add 2 eggs, 2 T. sage, ½ tsp. ground cloves and 1 T. salt. Bake in oven at 350° until the dressing is browned. This assures a tender, tasty coon without being too fat and greasy. Also good for possum.

How To Cook Coon

Cut up, boil in water with a little salt until tender. Place in shallow pan, sprinkle with a little sage, add one cup broth. Pre-cook about 5 medium size sweet potatoes, cut in half and place around coon. Bake in hot oven for 20 minutes.

Old Fashioned Coon

Put one coon in salt and soda water and let stand overnight. Take out of water next morning and wash two times and put in kettle and boil until tender. Put in a bread pan and put pepper and sage on it and bake. Serve with sweet potatoes.

Country Fried Chicken

This recipe is for two chickens and it can be adjusted to suit the amount. Cut chicken into pieces for frying and wash well. Roll in a mixture of: 2 C. flour, 4 tsp. salt and ¼ tsp. pepper. Put skillet on , put in about ½-inch of fat and get it hot. Place chicken in and fry till brown, turning often. Then reduce heat, cover well and cook about 25 minutes till tender. The leavings are mightly good make white sop (white milk) gravy.

Smother Chicken—Country Style

Cut up chicken, salt, roll each piece in flour and place in roaster. Lay 4 or 5 slices of bacon, ½ medium onion (sliced) and celery leaves on top. Cover with water and bake three hours.

Turtle Soup Or Stew

A delicious soup can be prepared the same as with a choice piece of beef or pork. A delicious stew can be made the same by adding the desired vegetables.

Meat Loaf

1 lb. ground beef	*1 T. melted butter*
¼ onion (finely chopped)	*1 egg (slightly beaten)*
1 C. cracker crumbs	*1 tsp. salt*
1 C. milk	*⅓ tsp. pepper*

Mix all ingredients together with the hands. Then again with the hands, form into loaf pan, add any extra seasonings desired and bake at 350° for about 1½ hours till done.

Pan Cakes

4 C. flour	*1 tsp. salt*
3 C. milk	*2 eggs*
4 level tsp. baking powder	*4 T. melted shortening*

Combine ingredients in mixing bowl. Beat until light. Cook on hot griddle.

Sourdough Pancakes

This is a two-part recipe. Th'furst part is for a "starter" an'th second is fer th' actual pancakes.

Starter:

1 package yeast	2 C. lukewarm potato water
1 tsp. sugar	2 C. flour
1 tsp. salt	

Soften yeast in the warm potato water. Mix all ingredients well in earthenware bowl and then set away in this bowl, loosely covered, to ferment. The batch will take 48 hours to ferment. After this period pour starter into jar with lid and keep in the refrigerator to be used as needed.

PANCAKES:

These pancakes must be mixed the night before they are cooked, so if you get a yen for some sourdough pancakes, don't forget, mix the following the night before.

2 C. "starter"	2½ C. flour
2 C. lukewarm water	1 T. sugar

Cover and let set in warm place overnight. In the morning, take out 2 C. of the mix and replace that taken out of the ''starter''. To the remainder add:

¼ C. evaporated milk	2 tsp. sugar
½ tsp. salt	3 T. oil
1 tsp. soda	2 eggs

After mixing well, let stand for few minutes, then cook on hot griddle. (For waffles; add 2 extra T. oil).

Old Time Buckwheat Cakes

1 pkg. yeast	¾ C. sweet milk
2 C. lukewarm water	¼ tsp. salt
1½ C. flour	1 C. buckwheat flour

Soak yeast in lukewarm water. Stir in flour (regular) and let set over night. Next morning add sweet milk, salt and buckwheat flour to make a thin batter. Fry on hot griddle and eat while hot. Good with sugar syrup.

Chicken Dumplings

1 fried chicken (cut in pieces)

DUMPLINGS:
2 C. flour   *½ tsp. salt*
2 tsp. baking powder   *Water*

Fry chicken in skillet until brown. Make a thin gravy and then add to the chicken and simmer until done. Add the dumplings last.

For Dumplings: Mix the flour, baking powder and salt and enough water for stiff dough. Drop by spoonfuls on top of pieces of fried chicken and gravy in skillet. Cover with lid and do not take lid off. Simmer for 15 minutes.

Chicken-Noodle Scallop

1 can cream of chicken soup   *1½ C. diced cooled chicken*
½ C. milk   *¼ C. chopped onion*
1¾ C. frozen peas   *¼ tsp. paprika*
1½ C. cooked noodles   *Dash pepper*

Mix soup and milk, bring to boil. Remove from heat. Add peas, noodles, onion, chicken, paprika and pepper. Mix well. Pour into 1½ qt. baking dish; top with ¼ C. buttered bread crumbs. Bake at 350° for 35-40 minutes. Serve 4.

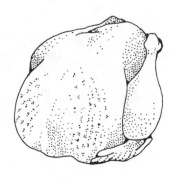

Stuffed Roast Beef

This requires a piece of ribs which have been boned, so you will have to do the boning or get your butcher to do so. Prepare a nice, turkey dressing. Unroll the beef; spread the dressing as thick as it will admit; roll it up, tie it firmly and roast as other roast beef. A joint of beef boned can be prepared the same way. This requires more gravy than a usual roast. Slice it around, not lengthwise.

Beef And Pork Loaf

2 lbs. ground beef
1 lb. ground pork
2 C. bread crumbs
½ C. chopped onion
1 T. salt

1 egg
1 C. milk
¼ tsp. pepper
¼ C. tomato catsup

Mix all ingredients thoroughly in large bowl. Put in loaf pan, cover with mixture of ½ C. catsup and 2 T. brown sugar and bake in moderate oven (350°) one hour.

Chicken Breasts

8 chicken breasts (boneless)   *1 can mushroom soup*
8 strips bacon   *1 can mushrooms*
2 pkgs. dried beef   *1½ C. sour cream*

Wrap breasts with bacon and secure with toothpicks; tear dried beef in pieces and spread on bottom of a 9 × 13-inch pan. Lay breasts on dried beef and pour soup and sour cream mixed together over top and add mushrooms on top. Bake in slow oven at 325° for 2-2½ hours.

Skillet Taters

Peel and dice about 5 potatoes and place in skillet with ¼ C. butter. Chop coarsely about 1½-2 C. onions and dump in with the potatoes. Then add 2 T. minced parsley, 2 T. minced green pepper and salt and pepper to taste. Fry till brown while stirring once in a while. Serve hot.

Catfish Balls

Bake or steam catfish. (Modern method is to cook in a pressure cooker.) Remove fish from bones and flake. To every 2 C. flaked fish add 2 C. mashed potatoes, 1 egg, salt and pepper to taste. Shape in balls and fry in deep fat.

Sweet Corn Griddle Cakes

1 pt. grated corn
1 C. flour
1 T. melted butter
4 eggs

1 tsp. salt
1 tsp. baking powder
Milk

Combine corn, flour, melted butter, eggs, salt and baking powder with enough milk to make a batter of the right consistency. Cook on hot griddle.

Possum And Chestnuts

Skin possum, remove glands and entrails. Scrape clean and scald in boiling water. Rub inside and out with salt and pepper and set in cool place. Stuff with chestnuts, apple sauce and bread crumbs in equal proportions. Cover with slices of sweet potato one cup boiling water, one-half cup lemon juice. Bake in butter and baste often until tender.

Possum

Take a possum and parboil until tender. Take out of water and put in bread pan, then pepper to taste. Take three large sweet potatoes and boil until tender. Lay these around possum in bread pan, put in oven and bake until brown. Serve warm.

How To Fix Bony Fish

After fish is dressed, carve cross-wise with a sharp knife. Salt to taste and roll in flour and corn meal mixed equally. Put in hot fat and fry until brown. Put in inset pans and set in pressure cooker with one-half inch of water in bottom of cooker. Cook for 45 minutes with 15 lbs. pressure. Fish cooked this way is good warmed over in hot fat in open skillet.

Sweet Corn Dish

12 ears corn

1 T. sugar

1 qt. rich milk

Salt

2 T. flour

1 T. butter

3 eggs

Grate the corn and mix it in the milk, rubbing well to get hulls free. Then rub through a fine seive to get rid of hulls. Work the flour and butter ot a cream, then beat in the sugar and well-beaten yolks. Then add the beaten whites; add all to the corn and milk mixture, with salt to taste. Bake. Eat as side dish or with cream and sugar as pudding.

Stuffed Peppers

6 greens peppers

2 C. chopped chicken or veal

3 T. butter

⅔ C. butter crumbs

3 T. flour

½ tsp. salt

1½ C. milk or cream

Onion juice

Cut top from the peppers; remove carefully all the seeds and tongue. Cut thin slices from the bottoms so the peppers will stand. Melt the butter; add the flour and seasoning, then the milk and onion juice; add the meat and fill the peppers with the mixture. Cover with crumbs made by stirring ⅔ C. bread crumbs into ⅔ T. of melted butter. Place the peppers in a baking pan and cover the bottom with boiling water. Bake in a moderate oven for 30 minutes.

Baked Carp

Choose fresh clear, cold water carp and skin the same as catfish. Cut up as if to fry. Choose size of roaster to suit amount of fish, then put in a layer of fish rolled in flour with salt and pepper. Then add a layer of bacon strips, then another layer of fish etc., topping with a layer of smoked bacon strips. Bake and serve warm.

Tater Puffs

2 C. mashed potatoes
2 T. butter
Salt and pepper

2 eggs (beaten separate)
½ C. cream

Combine and work all ingredients together. Form into the size of balls desired. Bake in oven till brown or fry in deep fat.

Chicken Strata

8 slices day old bread
2 C. diced cooked chicken
½ C. chopped onion
½ C. green pepper
½ C. finely chopped celery
½ C. mayonnaise

¾ tsp. salt dash pepper
2 slightly beaten eggs
1½ C. milk
2 cans cream mushroom soup
(condensed)
½ C. shredded sharp American
cheese

Butter 2 slices bread, cut in ½-inch cubes and set aside. Cut remaining bread in 1-inch cubes. Place half of unbuttered cubes in bottom of 9-inch baking dish. Combine chicken, vegetables, mayonnaise and seasonings. Spoon over bread cubes. Sprinkle remaining unbuttered cubes over chicken mixture. Combine eggs and milk; pour over all. Cover and chill 1 hour or better overnight. Spoon soup over top. Sprinkle with buttered cubes. Bake at 325° oven 1 hour or until set. Sprinkle cheese over top last few minutes of baking. Makes 6-8 servings.

Tater Cakes Or Balls

1 qt. mashed potatoes (hot)
½ C. hot milk
Whites of 2 eggs

2 heaping T. butter
1 tsp. salt
Yolks of 2 eggs

To 1 qt. of hot mashed potatoes, add hot milk, butter, salt and beat well. Beat the egg whites stiff and stir in. Form into patties or balls, roll in the egg yolks and then in cracker crumbs. Fry in deep hot fat.

Pan Fried Fish

Scale and clean fish well and wash very good in cold water. If small, fry them as is. If large, cross-slit them along side so they will cook better. Salt them and then roll in flour and meal mixed equally. Fry in ½ to 1 inch of hot fat. Turn and brown on both sides. Serve hot.

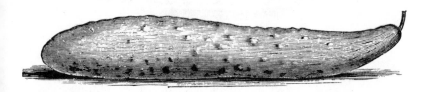

Fried Cucmbers

Pare cucumbers and cut length-wise in very thick slices; wipe them dry with a cloth; sprinkle with salt and pepper and dredge with flour. Fry in pan greased with about a 1 T. each of lard and butter. Brown both sides and serves warm.

Corn Pudding

2 C. raw corn (cut and milked   1 T. flour
   from ears)   Pinch of salt
⅔ C. heavy cream   Pinch of pepper

Mix well. Pour into greased 4 C. casserole. Bake 1 hour at 350°.

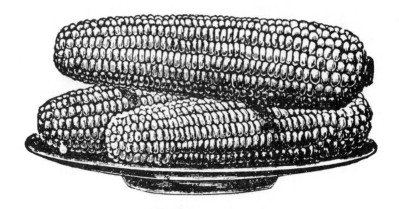

Corn Meal Mush

Put two quarts of water into a clean dinner pot or stew pan, cover it and let it become boiling hot over the fire; then add a tablespoon of salt, take off the light scum from the top. Using sweet, yellow or white corn meal; take a handful of the meal with the left hand and a pudding stick in the right; then with the stick, stir the water around and by degrees let fall the meal. When one handful is exhausted, refill it: continue to stir and add meal until it is as thick as you can stir easily. When it is sufficiently cooked, which will be in about ½ hour, it will bubble or puff up. Now turn into a deep basin. This is eaten cold or hot, with milk or with butter and syrup or sugar, or with meat and gravy, the same as potatoes or rice.

Bakin' Taters Twice

Bake potatoes as usual once. Cut open, but do not part halves. Scoop out middle; add butter and milk to it and whip. Before finished whipping; add seasonings desired. Pile it back in shells, place favorite cheese on top and bake till golden brown. Garnish top as desired and serve.

Buttermilk Waffles

2 C. flour
4 eggs (separtaed)
1½ C. buttermilk
¼ C. shortening (melted)

2 tsp. baking powder
½ tsp. baking soda
¾ tsp. salt
1½ T. sugar

Place egg yolk in bowl, beat well, then add shortening and buttermil. Add all other ingredients (except egg whites), mix well. Beat egg white stiff, then fold in. Cook in waffle iron.

Meat Loaf Dish

1½ lbs. ground beef
¾ C. dry bread crumbs
1 C. milk
¼ C. grated onion

2 eggs (beaten)
½ tsp. sage
1 tsp. salt
1/8 tsp. pepper

Soak bread crumbs in milk, then blend with remainder of ingredients; place in baking dish. Cover with sauce made by mixing: ¼ C. catsup, 3 T. brown sugar, 1 tsp. dry mustard and ⅓ tsp. nutmeg. Bake for about 60 minutes at 350°.

Spanish Meat Sauce

1 finely chopped onion
2 T. butter
1 red pepper
¼ tsp. celery salt
1 green pepper

1 clove of garlic
2 tomatoes (peeled, chopped)
1 tsp. Worcestershire sauce
Salt

Cook onion in butter for 5 minutes. Add other ingredients, except seasonings. Cook for 15 minutes, then season.

Baked Corn

1 C. cream style corn
½ C. milk
1 egg (beaten)

¼ C. sugar
2 T. flour
Salt and pepper

Combine all ingredients, blend in well and pour into a baking dish. Bake at 350° for 45-60 minutes.

Crispy Baked Fillets

1 lb. fish fillets (your choice)
Season salt
Lemon and pepper seasoning

2 T. oil
⅓ C. corn flake crumbs

Preheat oven to 500°. Wash and dry fillets and cut into serving pieces. Season and dip in oil and coat with corn flake crumbs. Arrange in a single layer in a lightly oiled shallow baking dish. Bake 10 minutes without turning.

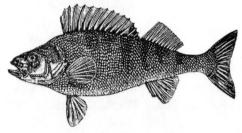

Apple Flapjacks

2 eggs (well beaten)
1½ C. flour
1 C. apples (chopped fine)
Milk

1 tsp. baking powder
1 T. sugar
1 T. shortening
1 tsp. cinnamon

Combine sugar and shortening; cream together. Add flour, baking powder, cinnamon, eggs and apples, mix well. Add enough milk to make a stiff batter. Cook on greased hot griddle.

Buttermilk Pancakes

2 eggs (beaten)
1½ C. buttermilk
1 C. water
2 C. flour
3 T. sugar

1½ tsp. baking soda
6 tsp. baking powder
1 tsp. salt
2 T. butter (melted)

Combine eggs, buttermilk and water, beat well. Combine flour, sugar, baking soda, baking powder and salt, add to liquid mix and mix well. Mix in butter. Cook on hot greased griddle.

Maid-Rite Hamburger Mix

1½ lbs. ground beef
1 tsp. salt

1/8 tsp. pepper
1 can chicken gumbo soup

Set electric skillet at 350°. Cook and stir meat until crumble and light brown. Add salt, pepper and soup; simmer at 190° for 15-20 minutes. Serve on buns with mustard dill pickles and sliced onion.

Buckwheat Cakes

2 C. buckwheat flour
1 C. flour
1 T. molasses
Water

4 C. water
1 pkg. yeast
1 tsp. salt
1 tsp. baking soda

Night before: Dissolve yeast in 4 C. warm water. Add buckwheat flour, flour, molasses and salt, mix well and let set in a warm place. Morning: Dissolve baking soda in a litle hot water; add to batch with just enough water to make a good batter. Cook on a hot greased griddle.

Barbecue Beef Sandwiches

3-4 lbs. beef roast (cooked & sliced)
2½ C. ketchup
½ C. brown sugar
½ C. vinegar

1 T. horseradish
1 T. Worcestershire sauce
1 tsp. garlic salt

Mix all ingredients, except beef and bring to a boil, then simmer for about 15 minutes. Pour over beef and place in oven or microwave until beef is thoroughly warmed. Serve on buns.

GARLIC

Mashed Potato Rolls

6 C. flour
1 C. mashed potatoes
½ C melted shortening
¾ C. sugar
1 C. hot milk

3 eggs
1 tsp. salt
2 pkgs. yeast
¼ C. lukewarm water

Dissolve yeast in ¼ C. lukewarm water. Beat eggs well; add yeast, sugar, potatoes and salt, mix well. Add flour in slowly, mixing and kneading as you go. Knead very well, at least 10 minutes. Cover dough in greased container and let sit to rise until double, then punch down. Roll out, cut form into rolls, and place on baking pan. Let rise again. Bake for about 15 minutes at 400°.

Chicken Sandwich Filling

1½ C. chopped chicken
¼ C. chopped pickle
1 tsp. Worcestershire sauce

⅓ C. undiluted cream of chicken
   soup
¼ tsp. celery (salt or powder)

Mix together all ingredients. Makes enough for 6 sandwiches.

Corn Pone

Take 4 C. corn meal, add enough cold water to make a soft dough. Add 1 tsp. salt and 2 T. melted shortening, mix well. Shape into cakes with hands, place on well-greased pans and bake in a very hot oven.

Chicken Dressing

3 lbs. chicken	1 T. celery salt
3 loaves bread	2 T. sage
6 eggs	4 tsp. salt
3 C. chicken broth	3 C. fresh ground onions
¾ T. pepper	2 C. finely chopped celery

Simmer chicken with celery leaves until done. Remove chicken to cool. Save broth. Remove skin and bones from chicken and put chicken through meat grinder. Cube bread slices. Dampen thoroughly with water and squeeze dry. Beat eggs; add chicken broth, pepper, celery salt, sage and salt. Beat together the egg mixture ingredients, then add bread and mix to a fine consistency. Add ground onions, chopped celery and the ground chicken. Mix again, then generously butter large roaster and pour in dressing. Preheat oven to 350°. Bake dressing 2½-3 hours or until firm. Baste occasionally with chicken broth. The recipe serves 25 people.

Rhubarb Pizza

1 C. flour	3 C. rhubarb (cut up)
1 tsp. baking powder	1 (3 oz.) pkg. cherry Jello
¼ tsp. salt	½ C. flour
2 T. butter	⅓ C. butter
1 egg	1 C. sugar
2 T. milk	

Mix 1 C. flour, baking powder and salt; cut in butter. Beat the egg and milk together and add to make batter for the crust. Press in bottom of 9-inch square pan. Spread rhubarb over dough. Sprinkle dry Jello over rhubarb. Mix flour, sugar and melted butter for topping and sprinkle on top. Bake 40-45 minutes at 350°.

BREADS

Breads

Breads - Continued

"Just For Notes"

Gingerbread

½ C. butter
1 C. sugar
3 C. flour (sifted)
1 C. molasses
1 C. sour milk
¼ C. hot water

2 eggs (beaten)
2 tsp. ginger
2 tsp. cinnamon
¼ tsp. nutmeg
1 tsp. baking soda
1 tsp. ginger

Cream butter and sugar. Add eggs slowly, beat as you add. Combine molasses and water, then mix in batch slowly. Combine all dry ingredients; add this mix alternately with sour milk, mixing well as you do. Grease bottom of pan, pour batter in and bake for about 35 minutes in 350° oven until tests done. I like this served warm with a cold glass of milk.

Dried Apple Stack Cake

CAKE RECIPE:
1 C. sugar
1 C. shortening
1 C. sorghum molasses
¼ C. buttermilk
1 egg
Flour (about 5 C.)

2 tsp. soda in 1 T. spoon vinegar
½ tsp. salt
1 tsp. cinnamon
½ tsp. ginger

Cream sugar, shortening, sorghum, then add egg and buttermilk, mix well. Stir in dry ingredients together with vinegar-soda mixture. Divide dough in-to 6 balls, press each ball of dough into well greased 8-inch cake pan. Bake in 350° oven 15 minutes or until slightly browned. Remove from pans while warm and set aside to cool.

To Make Filling:
1 qt. (cooked) home dried apples   4 T. cream

Drain dried apples and sweeten to taste. Mash apples and add cream to make a thin paste. Spread apple mixture between cake layers, leave top plain. Let stand at least 12 hours before serving.

Buttermilk Biscuits

2 C. flour
⅔ C. buttermilk
¼ C. bacon drippings
2 T. melted butter

⅓ tsp. baking soda
1 tsp. baking powder
¾ tsp. salt

Combine flour, baking soda, baking powder and salt, mix well. Add bacon drippings, stir in. Mix in milk slowly to a stiff dough. Knead lightly on floured board, roll out and cut. Place on greased pan, butter tops; bake until brown in 450° oven.

Alma's Sorghum Molasses Raisin Bread

2 C. milk (scalded and hot)
2 T. melted shortening
¼ C. molasses

¾ C. raisins
1½ tsp. salt
1 cake yeast
6 C. flour

Combine milk, shortening and molasses in mixing bowl and let cool till lukewarm. Add yeast and then allow to stand for about 5 minutes. Then add raisins. Add flour, a little each time, you have stiff dough. It must be stiff enough to knead on a lightly floured board. Knead till smooth and elastic. Cover with warm damp cloth and let it rise to double in bulk again. Form into loaves with hands and place into well-greased pans. Cover and let the dough rise once more till double in bulk. Bake in a hot oven at about 415° for about 45 minutes or until done. Good served warm with coffee.

Honey Twist

When sweet yeast dough is light, form into a long roll about 1-inch in diameter. Coil the roll into a greased cake pan, beginning at the outside edge and covering the bottom. Brush with Honey Topping below. Let rise until double in bulk. Bake in moderate oven (350°) for 25-30 minutes.

¼ C. butter	⅔ C. powdered sugar
1 egg white	2 T. warm honey

Cream all ingredients together, brush twist before baking.

Potato Muffins

1 C. corn meal	2 T. veg oil
¾ C. milk	2 tsp. sugar
1 C. mashed potatoes	4 tsp. baking powder
1 egg (beaten)	1 tsp. salt

Combine egg, oil and potatoes, beat well. Add sugar and milk, mix and then sift in all dry ingredients, mix well. Bake in greased muffin pans for 30 minutes (until brown) in a moderate oven.

Apple Rolls

½ C. sugar
1¼ tsp. salt
¼ C. shortening
3¼ C. flour (sifted)
1 well beaten egg
2 C. apples (sliced)
Milk

2 pkgs. yeast (dissolved in ⅔ C.
    hot water
1 C. brown sugar
2 tsp. cinnamon
¼ C. melted butter
¾ C. powdered sugar

Blend together sugar, salt, shortening and egg; stir in yeast/water. Mix in flour; beat for 2 minutes. Set aside and let rise until double. Roll dough out in a rectangle, brush with melted butter and sprinkle with a mixture of brown sugar and cinnamon. Lay apple slices over dough; roll up tightly. Slice roll and lay pieces on greased pan, then let set to rise for 1 hour. Bake for 25 minutes at 400°. Glaze with a mixture of powdered sugar and enough milk to make just the right consistency.

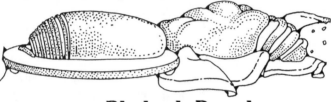

Rhubarb Bread

1½ C. brown sugar (firmly packed)
1 C. buttermilk
1 egg
⅔ C. veg oil
1 tsp. vanilla

2½ C. flour (sifted)
1 tsp. baking soda
1 tsp. salt
1½ C. fresh rhubarb
½ C. nutmeats (chopped)

Cream together sugar, buttermilk, egg, oil and vanilla. Combine dry ingredients; add to creamed mix, mix well. Stir in rhubarb and nutmeats. Pour into greased loaf pan. Bake about 1 hour at 350°, then:

Top with:
1½ C. sugar
1 T. butter

½ tsp. cinnamon

Combine and mix well. Sprinkle on bread while still hot.

Persimmon Bread

1½ C. sugar
½ C. cooking oil
2 C. flour (sifted)
2 beaten eggs
1 tsp. baking soda
¼ tsp. baking powder
1 C. persimmons (mashed)

½ tsp. cloves
½ tsp. cinnamon
½ tsp. nutmeg
½ tsp. allspice
1 tsp. salt
½ C. raisins

Combine sugar, oil and eggs, mix well. Add persimmons, baking soda, baking powder, spices and salt, mix well. Add flour slowly, mixing well as you do. Stir in raisins. Bake in loaf pans 50-60 minutes at 350° or until it tests done.

Peanut Butter Bread

2 C. flour
1 C. peanut butter
½ C. sugar
2 eggs (well beaten)

4 tsp. baking powder
1 tsp. salt
1 C. milk

Mix all ingredients well, pour into greased loaf pan, bake in moderate oven.

Fresh Apple Loaf

1½ C. sugar
2 beaten eggs
1 C. cooking oil
5 C. apples (chopped)
2½ C. flour (sifted)
1 C. nutmeats (chopped)

½ tsp. vanilla
1 tsp. baking soda
1 tsp. salt
1 tsp. cinnamon
1 tsp. nutmeg

Combine sugar, eggs, oil and vanilla, mix well. Combine flour, baking soda, salt and spices; mix into first mix. Stir in apples and nutmeats. Pour into buttered and floured loaf pan. Bake for 55-60 minutes at 350°.

Corn Bread

2 C. white meal (coarse ground
1 C. flour
1 T. sugar

Milk
4 tsp. baking powder
1 egg
1 tsp. salt

Combine all dry ingredients, then add egg and enough sweet milk to make thin batter. Pour in hot well grased bread pans or corn stick pans. Bake until brown in a hot oven. Mighty good with beans, sorghum, molasses or about anything.

Banana Bread

1 C. oleo
3 C. sugar
4 eggs
8 T. buttermilk

1 tsp. baking soda
½ tsp. salt
2 C. bananas (mashed)

Cream together oleo, sugar and eggs. Add dry ingredients and buttermilk slowly, mixing well as you add. Stir in bananas and nutmeats. Bake in greased loaf pans for 50-60 minutes at 350°.

Country Biscuits

In a bowl sift the following:

4 levels tsp. baking powder	*2 T. shortening*
1 tsp. salt	*1 C. flour*

Mix well, then add 1 C. milk and enough more flour to make a stiff batter. Pat out on floured board; cut and bake in very hot oven.

Whole Wheat Bread

2 pkgs. yeast	*6 T. shortening*
3 C. warm water	*4 C. unsifted stoneground whole*
4 C. white flour	*wheat flour*
4 T. white sugar	*2 C. pumpernickle rye flour*
2 T. salt	*2 C. additional white flour*
1 C. packed brown sugar	

Dissolve the yeast in the 3 C. warm water. Add flour, sugar and salt. Let rise in a warm place until light and bubbly, about 20 minutes. Combine the brown sugar, shortening and 1 C. of hot waer. Let cool to lukewarm and add to risen mixture. Add whole wheat flour, the pumpernickle rye flour and the remaining 2 C. of whtie flour. Mix as long as you can,then turn mixture onto table and knead for at least 15 minutes. Place in buttered bowl. Cover and let rise in warm place for 1 hour or until doubled in bulk. Turn onto a well floured table again and separate mixture into 4 balls. Cover and let stand for 15 minutes. Shape into 4 loaves. Place in greased bread pans. Let rise in pans, in warm place, covered with a towel, for about an hour or until light. Bake at 350° for 1 hour. Remove from pans and place on racks to cool. Butter top of bread while hot and store in plastic bags in refrigerator.

Pumpkin Roll

3 eggs
1 C. sugar
⅔ C. pumpkin
1 tsp. lemon juice
¾ C. flour

1 tsp. baking powder
2 tsp. cinnamon
1½ tsp. ginger
½ tsp. nutmeg
½ tsp. salt

FILLING:
1 C. powdered sugar
2 (3 oz. ea.) pkg. cream cheese

4 tsp. margarine
½ tsp. vanilla

Beat eggs for 5 minutes, gradually beating in sugar. Stir in pumpkin and lemon juice. Stir together flour, baking powder, cinnamon, ginger, nutmeg and salt. Fold into first mixture. Spread in greased and lightly floured jelly roll pan. Top with nuts and bake at 375° for 15 minutes. Immediately turn out on towel dusted with powdered sugar. Starting at narrow end, roll the towel. Cool. Unroll. For Filling: Combine powdered sugar, cream cheese, margarine and vanilla. Beat until smooth. Spread on roll; roll up and store in refrigerator.

Refrigerator Rolls

2 cakes yeast
¼ C. lukewarm wter
1 C. milk
½ C. light corn syrup

1 T. salt
2 eggs
½ C. melted shortening
6 C. flour

Soften the yeast in lukewarm water. Scald the milk; add the syrup and salt. Add 2 C. of flour and beat well. Add yeast. Beat the eggs and add them. Blend well and add the shortening and remaining flour to make a soft dough. Knead until smooth and satiny. Place in a lightly greased bowl. Grease top of dough. Cover well and put into refrigerator. When wanted remove dough form refrigerator and punch down. Mold at once in any desired shape or, if preferred let the dough stand in a warm room for an hour before molding. Place the rolls in greased pans and let them rise until dough in bulk. Bake in moderately hot oven (375°) from 15-20 minutes.

Squash Biscuits

1 pt. cooked, sieved squash
1 cake yeast
1 sm. C. sugar

½ tsp. salt
Butter size of an egg
Flour

Dissolve yeast in a little water. Add to the squash one cup sugar and the butter softened. Beat well, then turn in yeast, beat once more. Add sifted flour and stir well with a spoon. Add enough flour to make a stiff batter. Leave in a warm place over night. Then turn into greased gem pans and bake in a hot oven.

Grandma's Easy-Do Rolls

3 C. sifted flour
1½ tsp. soda
¾ tsp. salt
1 T. sugar
⅓ C. shortening

1 cake compressed or dry yeast
¼ C. lukewarm water
6 T. vinegar plus enough sweet
    milk to make ¾ C. liquid

Sift flour, baking soda, salt and sugar together and cut in shortening. Soften yeast in lukewarm water. Heat vinegar and milk to lukewarm and combine with yeast. Add liquid to dry ingredients gradually and stir only until flour is blended. Dough should be as soft as can be handled. Turn onto lightly floured board; knead gently one minute. Shape as desired. Place on lightly greased baking pan. Let rise an hour until doubled in bulk in warm place. Bake at 400° for about 15 mintues. Makes approximately 18 rolls.

Onion Bread

2½ C. flour
⅔ C. chopped onion
1 C. hot water
1 pkg. dry yeast
Flour

2½ tsp. sugar
2 tsp. salt
3 T. melted butter
2 tsp. paprika

Dissolve yeast with hot water in bowl. Add 2 C. flour, salt and sugar, beat well. Add remaining ½ C. flour, mix well. Turn out on floured board, knead until smooth. Add more flour if needed. Set aside in buttered bowl to rise until double in size. Punch down; place into butter pan. Spread melted butter over top, then push onions into top. Let rise again, then sprinkle paprika on top. Bake at 450° for about 20-25 minutes.

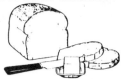

Mom's Hot Rolls

Combine: 2 pkgs. yeast, 1 tsp. sugar and 1 C. lukewarm water. Let stand for 10 minutes. Add:

1 C. warm water
5 T. sugar
2 tsp. salt

6 T. melted butter
6 C. flour or enough for a fairly
    stiff dough

Pour out on a floured dough board and knead well. Place in greased bowl and let rise in warm place until double in size. Then cut out, place on greased pan and let rise until double in size again. Bake in 400° oven until done.

Old Fashioned Biscuits

2 C. flour
2 tsp. baking powder
1 tsp. salt

¼ tsp. soda
2 T. shortening
¾ C. sour milk

Sift together flour, baking powder, salt and soda. Blend in shortening. Add sour milk and work lightly. Bake in well greased pan.

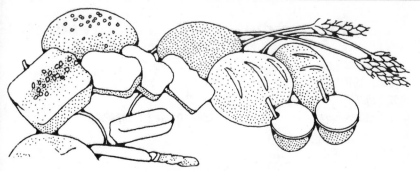

White Bread

2 C. milk
5 T. sugar
1½ T. salt
5 T. lard

2 C. lukewarm water
2 pkgs. yeast
12-13 C. flour

Scald milk and add lard, sugar and salt. Cool till lukewarm. Dissolve yeast in lukewarm water and add to lukewarm mixture. Beat in 6 C. flour until smooth. Gradually add remainder (6-7 C.) until dough forms a ball and is stiff enough to be kneaded. Turn out on floured board and knead quickly and lightly until smooth and elastic. Place in greased bowl, brush with melted lard or butter, cover and let rise until doubled, in warm place (will take 45 minutes to 1 hour). Divide dough into four equal protions and shape into loaves. Place in greased bread pans, cover and let rise until double in bulk, about an hour. Bake at 400° for about 50 minutes. Remove from pans and butter tops and sides.

Old-Fashioned Corn Bread

1½ C. buttermilk
1¼ tsp. soda
1 tsp. salt

1 egg
Cornmeal

Combine buttermilk, soda, salt and egg. Add enough corn meal to make the consistency of cake. Spoon this mixture out in a well greased pan and it will come out in small sections when baked. Bake in a moderate oven.

Great Grandma's Salt Risin Bread

3 medium potatoes
3 T. cornmeal
1 tsp. sugar
4 C. boiling water
Flour
2 C. lukewarm milk

1 C. water
1/8 tsp. soda
2 tsp. salt
2 T. melted shortening

Peel and slice potatoes; add cornmeal, sugar, salt and boiling water. Wrap the mixture in heavy cloth. Cover and allow to stand in a warm place over-night. Remove potatoes, add milk, water, soda, salt and shortening.Add enough flour to make dough stiff enough to knead until smooth and elastic. Then form into loaves. Place in well greased pans, cover and let rise until double in bulk. Bake in 400° oven until done. This makes 3 loaves.

Mush Biscuits

1 qt. hot water
Cornmeal
1 cake yeast
1 C. potato water

1 C. lard
1 C. sugar
1/8 tsp. salt
Flour

Take the hot water and make mush by adding enough cornmeal. Then dissolve yeast in warm water. Mix remaining ingredients together to make a sponge. Then add salt and stir in enough flour to make a stiff dough. Set to rise in a warm place. When double in bulk, roll out in biscuit form and bake in a moderate oven until brown.

Whole Wheat Bread

6 C. milk	2 pkgs. yeast
1 C. minus 2 T. sugar	¾ C. warm water
3 T. salt	5 C. whole wheat flour
¾ C. lard	12-14 C. white flour

Scald milk and add sugar, salt and lard. Cool to lukewarm. Dissolve yeast in warm water. Add yeast to milk mixture. Add whole wheat flour and stir. Add about half of the white flour and stir. Add remaining white flour and stir. Add enough of flour to make a dough that won't stick to hands. Turn dough onto floured board or counter. Cover and let rest for 10 minutes. Knead dough for 10 minutes. Put in greased bowl. Cover and let rise in warm place until doubled, about 1½ hours. Punch down and let rise again until doubled, about 1 hour. Make into 6 loaves to fit 3 or the 8½ × 4½ × 2½-inch pans and 3 of the 9½ × 5¼ × 2¾-inch pans (greased pans). Let rise until doubled in bulk, about 1½ hours. Bake at 400° for 10 minutes. Reduce to 325° and bake for 40 minutes.

Aunt Ida's Cracklin' Corn Bread

1½ C. white cornmeal	½ tsp. baking powder
1 C. buttermilk	½ tsp. baking soda
1 C. cracklings (fine chopped)	½ tsp. salt

Place cornmeal in bowl. Sift in flour, baking powder, baking soda and salt, mix well. Stir in milk, then cracklings. Pour into greased pan; bake at 450° for 30-35 minutes until brown.

All Kinds Of Bread

1 pkg. dry yeast
¼ C. warm water
1 C. milk
½ C. lard
½ C. sugar

1 T. salt
1 C. lukewarm water
6 C. flour
1 egg

Dissolve yeast in warm water. Heat milk and add lard, sugar, salt and lukewarm. Cool to lukewarm. Beat in 2 C. flour and egg. Add yeast mixture, then 3 C. flour mix and then remaining 1 C. flour. Knead lightly and rise until double. When light punch down and use to make donuts, pull apart, crescent rolls, knots, breadsticks, caramel rolls, cloverleafs, hamburger buns and bread rings. Bake at 350° until lightly brown.

Batter Bread

1 qt. sweet milk
1 pt. white cornmeal
3 eggs

1 T. melted butter
½ tsp. salt

Bring milk to a full boil and stir in slowly the cornmeal. Cool. Then add well beaten yolks of 3 eggs, melted butter and salt; then add the stiffly beaten whites of the eggs. Bake in a moderate oven at 375° until done.

Cracklin' Corn Bread

1½ C. cornmeal
½ C. flour
2 tsp. baking powder
½ C. cracklin's

½ tsp. salt
1 egg (beaten)
1½ C. milk

Sift together cornmeal, flour, baking powder and salt. In another bowl combine beaten egg, milk and the cracklin's. Combine with dry ingredients, beat well and pour into greased pan. Bake in a moderate oven until done. Should be brown.

Raisin Bread

2 pkgs. yeast
¼ C. warm water
1 .C raisins (soaked)
¼ C. soft margarine
¼ C. sugar

1½ tsp. salt
½ C. scalded milk or 4 T. dry milk
½ C. hot water
3¾ C. sifted flour
2 eggs (beaten)

Dissolve yeast in warm water. In mixing bowl, put raisins, margarine, sugar, salt and milk. Stir until sugar is dissolved. Ad yeast mixture to eggs and flour. Stir and work. Cover and let rise. Stir down when doubled in size and shape into 2 loaves. Let rise until loaf shape. Bake at 350° for 50-60 minutes.

Mom's Braided Bread

2 C. scalded milk
½ C. shortening
⅔ C. sugar
2 tsp. salt

2 pkgs. yeast
½ C. lukewarm water
2 eggs (beaten)
8 C. flour

Combine milk, shortening, sugar and salt. Cool to lukewarm. Add yeast, dissolved in water and mix well. Add eggs and stir. Add flour and mix well. Cover mixing bowl and let rise until double in bulk. Punch down and knead lightly. Divide dough into 3 parts. Next divide each 3 times (to make 3 braided loaves). Roll each of the 9 pieces of dough into a rope shape. Spread each rope generously with butter, cinnamon and sugar before braiding ropes together. Braid 3 ropes together to make 1 loaf. Let rise until double in bulk. Bake at 300° for 25-30 minutes. Ice with frosting made from milk, butter, powdered sugar and almond flavoring. Garnish with pecans, red and green cherries and candied fruit. Makes 3 loaves.

Whole Wheat Bread

⅔ C. warm water
2 pkgs. yeast
1 tsp. brown sugar
2 T. shortening
½ C. brown sugar

1 tsp. salt
2 C. hot water
3 C. whole wheat flour
3 C. white flour

Mix first 3 ingredients in a small dish and let stand until bubbly, then mix the shortening, ½ C. brown sugar, 1 tsp. salt and 2 C. hot water. Stir in whole wheat flour and beat well. Mix in white flour, 1 C. at a time, beating well after each addition. It may not take all the flour. When it is stiff enough to knead, pour out on floured board, cover and let set or ''rest'' for 10-15 minutes. Knead until no longer sticky (about 10 minutes). Let rise till double, punch down and shape into 2 loaves. Let rise again and bake at 350° for 50-60 minutes.

Bread Dough

½ C. milk	2 pkgs. yeast
½ C. sugar	½ C. water
1 tsp. salt	3 eggs
¼ C. butter	4½ C. flour

Scald milk; stir in sugar, salt and butter. Dissolve yeast in warm water; add milk, eggs, and half of the flour. Beat well and add enough flour to make soft dough. Knead until smooth. Let rise for 1 hour. Shape into loaves or rolls; let rise. Bake at 350° until done.

White Bread

½ C. warm water	5 T. sugar
½ tsp. sugar	1 tsp. salt
2 pkgs. yeast	2 T. lard
2 more C. warm water	5½ C. flour

Dissolve yeast in the ½ C. warm water with ½ tsp. sugar. Mix the 2 C. warm water with sugar, salt, melted (or soft) lard and stir in dissolved yeast. Beat in flour, 2 C. at first, then add 1 C. at a time until dough is stiff enough to turn out on floured board. Let rest for 10 minutes and then knead until smooth and elastic. Put in greased bowl and cover, let rise in warm place until doubled in bulk. Shape into 3 loaves, put in greased bread pans, cover and let rise until doubled or light. Bake at 350-375° for 30-40 minutes until nicely browned.

Oatmeal Muffins

1½ C. sifted flour	¼ C. shortening or margarine
½ C. brown sugar	1 C. rolled oats
2½ tsp. baking powder	1 egg
¾ tsp. soda	1¼ C. buttermilk or sour milk
¾ tsp. salt	

Sift together flour, sugar, baking powder, soda and salt. Cut in shortening until mixture is in coarse crumbs. Stir in oats. Add egg and buttermilk, stirring just until ingredients are moistened. Fill greased or paper cup-lined muffin cups two-thirds full. Bake at 425° for 18-20 minutes.

Rich Dinner Rolls

1 C. milk	½ C. warm water
¼ C. sugar	2 pkgs. dry yeast
1 tsp. salt	2 eggs (beaten)
¼ C. margarine	5¼ C. flour (unsifted)

Scald milk and stir in sugar, salt and margarine. Cool to lukewarm. Measure warm water into large warm bowl. Sprinkle or crumble in yeast and stir until dissolved. Add lukewarm milk mixture, eggs and 2 C. of flour. Beat until smooth. Stir enough remaining flour to make soft dough. Turn out onto lightly floured board. Knead until smooth and elastic, about 8-10 minutes. Place in greased bowl, turning to grease top. Cover and let rise in warm place free from draft, until doubled in bulk, about 30 minutes. Punch down and turn out on lightly floured board. This dough can be made into pan rolls, crescent and cloverleaf rolls.

Spoon Rolls

1 pkg. yeast
¼ C. lukewarm water
¼ C. sugar
1 tsp. salt
⅓ C. shortening

¾ C. scalded milk
½ C. cold water
1 egg
3½ C. flour

Dissolve yeast in lukewarm water. Combine sugar, salt, shortening and scalded milk in a large bowl. Cool to lukewarm by adding ½ C. cold water. Blend in 1 egg and the dissolved yeast. Add sifted flour to mixture and mix until well blended. Place in greased bowl and cover with a towel. Let rise in a warm place until double in bulk, about 45-60 minutes. Stir down dough. Spoon into well-greased muffin tins, filling ½ full. Let rise in warm place until batter has risen to edge of muffin cup and is rounded in center, about 45 minutes. Bake in medium-hot, 400° for 15-20 minutes. Makes 18 rolls.

English Oat Muffins

1 C. boiling water
¼ C. brown sugar (firmly packed)
¼ C. vegetable oil
1 pkg. dry yeast
3-3½ C. flour

1 C. quick roll oats
1 tsp. salt
1 egg
¼ C. water
Cornmeal

In a large mixer bowl, pour boiling water over rolled oats. Stir in brown sugar, salt and oil. Cool to lukewarm. Dissolve yeast in warm water. Beat yeast and egg into oat mixture. Stir in enough flour to make a moderately stiff dough. Cover and let rest in warm place for 30 minutes (dough does not double). Turn out on lightly floured surface and roll to ¾-inch thickness. Cut into rounds with a 3-inch cutter. Place on greased baking sheets. Sprinkle with cornmeal. Cover and let rise in warm place until doubled, about 45 minutes. Bake on lightly greased griddle over medium heat for 20 minutes, turning every 5 minutes. Yield: 16-18.

Cottage Cheese Muffins

1½ C. sifted flour
¼ C. sugar
4 tsp. baking powder
1 tsp. salt
1 C. small curd creamed cottage
   cheese
⅓ C. vegetable oil

½ tsp. soda
1 C. cornmeal
1½ C. whole wheat flour
2 eggs
1 C. buttermilk

Stir together flour, sugar, baking powder, salt and soda. Stir in cornmeal and whole wheat flour. In small bowl beat eggs. Stir in cottage cheese, buttermilk and oil. Make a well in dry ingredients. Add egg mixture stirring just enough to moisten (batter will be lumpy). Spoon into 24 greased muffin tins. Bake at 400° for 20-30 minutes.

Apple Bread

½ C. butter
1 C. sugar
2 eggs
1 tsp. vanilla
1 tsp. soda

TOPPING:
2 T. flour
2 T. sugar

½ tsp. salt
2 T. sour milk
2 C. diced apples
2 C. flour

1 tsp. cinnamon
2 T. melted butter

Cream together butter, sugar, eggs, vanilla and salt. Dissolve soda in sour milk, then add apples and flour. Add nuts, if desired. Put in 2 small or 1 large greased and floured loaf pan, then mix together butter, flour, sugar and cinnamon. Sprinkle on top of batter. Bake at 325° for 1 hour.

Bran Muffins

3 C. unprocessed bran
1 C. boiling water
2 eggs
⅓ C. corn oil
⅔ C. brown sugar

2 C. buttermilk
2½ C. whole wheat flour
1 tsp. cinnamon
2½ tsp. baking soda
½ C raisins

Pour boiling water over bran and set aside. Beat eggs, oil and sugar together. Add buttermilk, baking soda and cinnamon; beat. Add bran and flour; mix well. Add raisins. Store, covered in refrigerator for 12 hours. Fill Pam, greased muffin tins ⅔ full. Bake at 400° for 25 minutes. Makes 24 muffins. Mixture keeps in refrigerator for 6 weeks.

Rhubarb Muffins

1 C. sugar
¼ tsp. salt
3 T. margarine
2 eggs
¾ C. sour milk

1 tsp. vanilla
2½ C. flour
1 tsp. soda
1 C. raw rhubarb

Mix above ingredients well. Add 1 C. chopped raw rhubarb. Bake at 375° for 20-25 minutes. Makes 18-20 muffins.

"Just For Notes"

CAKES

Cakes

Cakes - Continued

"Just For Notes"

Refrig Coffee Cake

¾ C. oleo   1 C. white sugar
½ C. brown sugar   2 eggs

SIFT:
2 C. flour   1 tsp. baking powder
½ tsp. soda   1 tsp. nutmeg
½ tsp. salt

TOPPING:
½ C. brown sugar   1 tsp. cinnamon

Cream shortening, sugars and eggs. Sift dry ingredients together. Mix with creamed mixture. Add 1 C. of sour cream, also 1 C. of nuts, if desired. Pour into 9 × 13-inch greased pan. Sprinkle brown sugar and cinnamon over the top. Cover and refrigerate overnight. The next morning, preheat oven to 350° and bake for 35-40 minutes.

Burnt Sugar Cake

Brown ½ C. sugar   Add ¼ C. water

Let come to a light brown color. Cool.

1½ C. sugar   1 C. cold water
½ C. butter (or shortening)   2 C. flour
2 egg yolks   2 tsp. baking powder

Cream sugar, butter; add egg yolks, 1 C. cold water, 2 C. flour. Beat 5 minutes. Add 2 tsp. baking powder, ½ C. flour, 2 stiffly beaten egg whites, burnt sugar and 1 tsp. vanilla. Fold in. Bake at 350° for 30-35 minutes.

Oatmeal Cake

1¼ C. boiling water; pour over 1 C. quick oatmeal. Let stand 20 minutes.

ADD:

1 C. white sugar
1 C. brown sugar
½ C. shortening
2 eggs

1 tsp. vanilla
1½ C. flour
1 tsp. soda
¼ tsp. salt

TOPPING:

6 T. butter
1 C. brown sugar
4 T. condensed milk (Eagle Brand)

½ C. chopped nuts
1 C. coconut

Boil a few minutes, spread on cake. Cake is wonderful, very moist!

Coffee Cake

2½ C. flour
2 C. brown sugar
½ tsp. salt
⅔ C. shortening
3 tsp. baking powder

½ tsp. soda
½ tsp. cinnamon
½ tsp. nutmeg
1 C. milk
2 eggs (beaten)

Mix the first 4 ingredients together and save out ½ C. of it. Take what is left and add the rest of the ingredients. Put in a 9 × 13-inch pan and sprinkle the ½ C. of flour, brown sugar, salt and shortening over the top of it. Bake at 375° for 25-30 minutes.

Strawberry Cake Surprize

1 box white cake mix
⅓ C. melted shortening

½ pkg. frozen strawberries
½ C. cold water

Beat above ingredients 2 minutes, then add 4 unbeaten egg whites. Beat with electric mixer for 5 minutes. Bake 30 minutes at 350°. Use 9×13-inch glass baking dish.

FROSTNG:
1 box powdered sugar
½ C. drained frozen strawberries
½ C. melted oleo (not hot)

1-2 drops red coloring
½ tsp. vanilla

Cool cake thoroughly before frosting.

Strawberry Shortcake

2 (10 oz. ea.) pkgs. strawberries (thawed)

1 (3 oz.) pkg. strawberry Jello

BATTER:
½ C. Crisco
1½ C. sugar
3 eggs
1 tsp. vanilla

2¼ C. flour
3 tsp. baking powder
½ tsp. salt
1 C. milk

Grease 9 × 12-inch pan. Sprinkle 1 C. miniature marshmallows on bottom. Pour batter over marshmallows. Add strawberries on top. Bake 25 minutes at 350°.

Pineapple Upside Down Cake

2½ C. sifted cake flour
3 tsp. baking powder
¼ tsp. salt
½ C. shortening
1½ C. granulated sugar
2 eggs (well beaten)

1 tsp. vanilla
1 C. milk
¼ C. butter or margarine
½ C. firmly packed brown sugar
Canned pineapple slices (drained, see note)
Marashino cherries

Mix and sift flour, baking powder and salt. Cream shortening; gradually beat in granulated sugar; mix well. Add eggs and vanilla; beat thoroughly. Add sifted dry ingredients, alternately, a little at a time with the milk. Turn temperature control knob to 230° and put butter in skillet immediately. When melted, add pineapple lices. Add brown sugar mixture with cherry in center of each. Pour cake batter over fruit. Cover and bake 30-35 minutes or until the top is dry and springs back when lightly touched. Immediately invert skillet and remove cake on a serving platter. Makes 9 large servings. (NOTE: for a 10½-inch skillet, use pineapple from a 20 oz. can; average number of slices in a can is 10. For an 11½-inch skillet, use slices from a 30 oz. can; average number per can is 8. If desired, cut slices in ¼ and arrange.)

Strawberry Sheet Cake

1 pkg. white cake mix
½ of a 10 oz. pkkg. frozen
  strawberries
½ C. milk
1 T. flour

4 eggs
4 eggs
1 (3 oz.) pkg. strawberry Jello
¾ C. salad oil

Mix all ingredients together well and bake at 350° for 40-50 minutes in
9 × 13-inch pan; 25-30 minutes for a sheet cake pan. Cool, slightly and frost
with strawberry frosting.

FROSTING:
1 box powdered sugar
1 stick margarine (softened)

½ of 10 oz. pkg. frozen
  strawberries

Mix together and spread on slightly cooled cake.

Boiled Cake

1 C. brown sugar
1 C. raisins
½ C. shortening

1 tsp. cinnamon
1 C. boiled water
¼ tsp. cloves

Put on stove and let boil only for short time. While hot, add 1 tsp. soda.
When cool, add 1 egg well beaten and then add 1 ¼ C. flour. Bake at 350°
about 45 minutes.

Disappearing Cake

3 C. flour
2 C. sugar
3 eggs
1½ C. cooking oil
1 (8 oz.) can crushed pineapple
  (drained)

1 tsp. baking soda
1 tsp. salt
1 tsp. cinnamon
1 tsp. vanilla
2 C. mashed potatoes
1 C. nuts

Mix dry ingredients in a large bowl. Make a well in the center. Add eggs, pineapple, nuts, oil, vanilla and bananas. Stir. Do not beat. (Will take only a few stirs to mix.) Pour into a greased and floured tube pan. Bake at 350° for 75 minutes.

Pineapple Topping Or Frosting

2 eggs
1 stick margarine
1½ C. sugar

1½-2 T. flour
1 C. crushed pineapple (drained)

Cook until thick, then let stand to cool before adding 1½ C. coconut.

Orange Cake

1½ C. sugar
¾ C. shortening
3 eggs
1 tsp. salt
1½ C. buttermilk

1½ tsp. soda
2½ C. flour
1½ tsp. vanilla
1 C. raisins and rind of 1 orange
   (ground together)

Preheat oven to 350°. Grease and flour 9×13-inch pan. Mix all ingredients well in large bowl. Pour into pan. Bake until done, about 45 minutes.

For Topping: Mix ½ C. sugar with juice of one orange. Pour over baked cake and place back in oven for 5 minutes. Or use Orange Icing.

ORANGE ICING:
½ C. soft butter
3 C. powdered sugar

2 T. grated orange peel
3-4 T. orange juice

Victory Cake

2¼ C. sifted flour
2¼ tsp. baking powder
¼ tsp. salt
½ C. shortening

1 c. light corn syrup
2 eggs (unbeaten)
½ C. milk
1 tsp. vanilla

Sift flour, salt and baking powder together 3 times. Cream shortening until fluffy. Gradually beat in the sryup and beat hard until mixture is fluffy. Add ¼ C. of the flour, beating until well blended. Add eggs, 1 at a time, beating well after each addition. Add the remaining flour in thirds, alternately with milk, mixed with vanilla. Beat well after each addition. Bake in two 8-inch layer pans at 350° for 20-25 minutes. Cool for 5 minutes, then invert on cake rack.

Sponge Cake

4 eggs
4 T. milk or water
1 C. sugar
1 tsp. vanilla

2 tsp. baking powder
¼ tsp. salt
1 C. flour

Beat eggs until very light. Add liquid and add sugar gradually. Add remaining dry ingredients. Bake in moderate oven. (For jelly roll use water for liquid and for a loaf pan use the milk.)

Banana Nut Cake

3 tsp. baking powder
2 C. flour
½ C. shortening
2 beaten egg whites

2 beaten egg yolks
¾ C. milk
1 tsp. vanilla
1 C. sugar

Add baking powder, to flour and sift very well. Cream butter, add sugar gradually as you cream again until mix is light and fluffy. Add gradually egg yolks, flour and milk; beating each time till smooth. Add vanilla and fold in egg whites. Use two 9-inch pans (greased) and bake at 375° for about 30 minutes. After cooling, cover bottom layer with sliced bananas, then frosting (your choice), then next layer and then frost outside. Nuts in frosting is optional.

Sour Cream Coffee Cake

Batter: Mix 1 C. oleo, 1 C. sour cream, 2 C. flour, 1 tsp. baking powder and ¼ tsp. salt, mix well.

Filling: Mix well together 1 C. nutmeats, 1½ tsp. cinnamon and ¾ C. brown sugar.

Grease and flour bundt pan. Pour in ½ of batter, then ½ of filling, then repeat. Bake at 350° for 1 hour. It looks sticky and heavy. Let cool a bit and turn out to cool.

Eva's Coffee Cake

1½ C. flour
1 C. sugar
2 tsp. baking powder
½ tsp. salt

½ C. oil
2 eggs
1 (8 oz.) carton yogurt
    (pineapple or orange is best)

TOPPING:
1 C. coconut
¼ C. sugar

1 tsp. cinnamon

OR:
2 T. butter
2 T. brown sugar

2 T. flour
½ tsp. cinnamon

Mix flour, sugar, baking powder and salt together. Add oil, eggs and yogurt; stir until just mixed. Put in an 8×8-inch pan. Top with desired topping. Cook in the microwave oven for 8 or 9 minutes.

Apple Muffins

1¾ C. flour
½ C. sugar
⅓ C. brown sugar
¾ C. milk
¼ C. shortening
½ C. nutmeats (chopped)

2 tsp. baking powder
1 egg (well beaten)
1¼ C. apple (chopped)
1 tsp. cinnamon
½ tsp. salt

Combine flour, sugar, baking powder, salt, ½ tsp. cinnamon and milk; mix well. Mix in eggs shortening and apples. Put batter into greased muffin pan or cups. Stir together brown sugar, nutmeats and ½ tsp. cinnamon to sprinkle on top. Bake in 360° oven for about 20-25 minutes.

American Coffee Cake

4½ C. flour
1 tsp. salt
2 T. butter
1½ C. milk

4 tsp. baking powder
4 T. sugar
2 eggs

Sift flour; add baking powder, salt and sugar; sift three times. Chop butter in with spoon. Beat egg whites (with half egg shell of water add to each) until stiff; add yolks and beat in. Add milk and beat all together. Turn into two square pans and spread even; brush top with milk. Spread with the following: ½ C. flour, ½ C. sugar, 1 tsp. cinnamon and 1 T. butter. Mix flour, sugar and cinnamon, rub butter in until it is crumbly, then spread thick on top of cakes. Bake in moderate oven 30-35 minutes.

Sour Cream Devils Food Cake

1 C. sour cream
1½ C. sugar
2 eggs (well beaten)
½ C. cocoa
½ C. hot water

1 T. butter
1 tsp. baking soda
2 C. flour (sifted)
1 tsp. vanilla

Dissolve cocoa in hot water. Combine sour cream and sugar, mix well. Mix in eggs. Add butter and cocoa water; mix well. Slowly mix in flour and vanilla. Stir in vanilla. Pour in greased and floured pan; bake until tests done in a 350° oven.

Hoecake

2 C. corn meal
½ tsp. salt

½ tsp. baking powder
1 T. melted fat

Combine 2 C. corn meal and ½ tsp. each of salt and baking powder. Add 1 T. melted fat and stir in water to make a soft dough. Make into small cakes about half an inch thick and bake on a hot greased griddle until brown and then turn to brown on other side.

Mom's Chocolate Cake

1 tsp. soda
½ C. boiling water
2 heaping T. cocoa
2 C. flour
2 C. sugar

½ C. shortening
2 eggs
1 tsp. salt
1 tsp. vanilla
1 C. buttermilk

Combine soda, boiling water and cocoa; set aside to cool. Cream together sugar and shortening, beat in eggs. Add dry ingredients and buttermilk alternately. Stir in vanilla and chocolate mixture (chocolate should be lukewarm) and pour into a well greased and floured pan. Bake at 350° for 25-30 minutes. This cake is very good warm with ''drippy icing''.

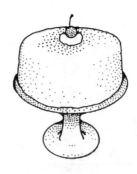

Huckleberry Cake

½ C. butter
1 C. sugar
3 eggs (beaten)
¾ C. milk

2 C. flour
2 tsp. baking powder
1 C. huckleberries

Cream butter with sugar. Add eggs and milk. Sift together flour and baking powder and add to mixture. Stir in a cup of huckleberries dredged with flour. Bake in a moderate oven (350°) in a deep cake pan. Serve plain or with vanilla sauce.

Aunt Bessie's Oat Meal Cake

1 C. oats (quick)
1¼ C. hot water
1 stick oleo
1 C. white sugar
1 C. brown sugar

2 eggs
1⅓ C. flour
1 tsp. soda
1 tsp. cinnamon
1½ tsp. salt

Pour oats over hot water and let stand for 20 minutes. Cream butter and sugar; add oatmeal-water mixture. Then sift in dry ingredients. Mix well. Pour into a greased and floured pan that measures about 9 × 13. Bake 35-40 minutes at 350°.

Apple Sauce Cake

2 C. brown sugar
1 C. butter
2½ C. flour
2 C. apple sauce
1 C. raisins
1 C. nutmeat (your choice)

1 tsp. soda
1 tsp. cinnamon
1 tsp. allspice
1 tsp. nutmeg
¼ tsp. salt

Cream butter and sugar together. Add apple sauce, raisins and nut meats. Sift flour, soda and spices together and add to mixture. Gradually beat after each addition. Bake in 375° oven for 30 minutes.

Wacky Cake

Mix the following ingredients together in a glass baking dish:

1½ C. flour
3 T. cocoa
5 T. shortening
1 C. water

1 tsp. soda
1 C. sugar
1 tsp. vanilla
1 T. vinegar
Pinch of salt

Mix well and pour into a well greased and floured baking pan. Bake at 250° until done, 40 or 50 minutes.

Cornmeal Balls

½ C. cornmeal
2 tsp. salt
2 C. milk
¾ C. sugar
¾ C. shortening

2 eggs (beaten)
2 pkgs. yeast
1 C. warm water
5-6 C. flour

Cook cornmeal, salt and milk until thick. While still hot add the sugar and shortening, cool. Dissolve yeast in warm water and mix well with cornmeal mixture. Add eggs and stir. Stir in 5-6 C. flour fo make medium dough. Knead, put in greased bowl and let rise for about an hour. Divide dough into 6 equal parts. Roll each part into a circle. Brush with melted butter. Cut into 8 pieces pie wedges. Start at large end to roll up and place on greased pan. Let rise for about 45 minutes. Bake at 350° for 12-15 minutes or until lightly brown.

Dried Apple Cake

2 C. dried apples
1 C. sugar
⅔ C. butter
2 tsp. baking powder
2 eggs
3 C. or more of flour

1 C. raisins
1 C. molasses
1 C. milk
1 tsp. soda (level)
Nutmeg and cinnmaon

Soak apples in water long enough to make soft. Then chip them to about the size of raisins and boil them for 15 minutes in the molasses. Dissolve the soda in a little hot water and put this in the molasses when cold. Then mix in all other ingredients, beat well and pour into cake pan. Bake in moderate oven till done.

Poor Man's Raisin Cake

1 C. raisins	1 C. sugar
2 C. water	2 C. flour
1 tsp. soda	1 tsp. baking powder
2 rounded T. shortening	

Pinch of each of the following: salt, allspice, nutmeg, cinnamon and ginger.

Cook raisins and water down to 1 C. juice. Add soda and shortening to liquid while warm. Add sugar and flour (enough to make light batter; not stiff), baking powder, salt, allspice, nutmeg, cinnamon and ginger. Mix well and bake at 350° until done.

Honey Bee Icing

1 C. sugar	½ C. honey
¾ C. marshmallow (chopped)	⅓ C. water
1 egg white (stiffly beaten)	1/8 tsp. salt
½ tsp. vanilla	

Combine together sugar, water and salt; place on stove. Boil to about 238° (soft ball) and add marshmallows. Beat and pour into beaten egg white very slowly. Add vanilla and beat until thick and creamy. Very good on most kinds of cake.

Vinegar Icing

¾ C. sugar (white)
1¼ C. brown sugar
2 egg whites (stiffly beaten)
1/8 tsp. cream of tartar

1½ T. vinegar
1 tsp. vanilla
¾ C. water

Combine white sugar, brown sugar, cream of tartar, vinegar and water in cooking pan. Mix together well and boil to about 238° (soft ball). Beat and pour slowly in stiffly beat egg whites; add vanilla, then beat until thick and creamy.

Coffee Icing

3½ C. powdered sugar
⅓ C. butter
3 T. cold coffee

2 T. lemon juice
Bit of salt

Cream butter and sift sugar into it. Add other ingredients and beat until smooth and creamy.

Banana Frosting

Mash one banana and place in mixing bowl. Add ⅓ C. butter. Cream together. Add 3 C. powdered sugar and ¼ tsp. vanilla. Beat till thick and creamy.

Johnny Cake

¾ C. flour
¾ tsp. salt
1 tsp. baking powder
1 tsp. baking soda

1⅓ C. yellow corn meal
2 eggs (well beaten)
1⅔ C. buttermilk
¼ C. melted shortening or
    salad oil

Combine first 5 ingredients. Stir in corn meal. Combine eggs, milk, shortening and add all at once to dry ingredients. Stir until just blended, but no longer. Put in pan, 11×7×½-inch and bake at 400° for 30-35 minutes. Cut in squares and serve hot.

Russian Tea Cakes

1 C. butter
2¼ C. sifted flour
1 tsp. vanilla

½ C. powdered sugar
¼ tsp. salt
¾ C. finely chopped nuts

Cream butter and powdered sugar. Add rest of ingredients. Bake on ungreased cookie sheet, teaspoon size balls, 14-17 minutes at 350°.

Coffee Cake

⅓ C. vegetable oil
1 egg
Milk
1 C. flour

1 C. sugar
1 tsp. baking powder
Pinch of salt

TOPPING:
⅓ C. brown sugar
1 tsp. cinnamon

Margarine (small amount)

Put vegetable oil and egg in 1 C. measuring cup, fill rest of cup with milk. Put in bowl, adding dry ingredients and mix well. Spread in 8×8-inch pan. Sprinkle with topping and bake at 350° for 25 minutes.

Coffee Cake

1 C. sugar
½ C. butter
1 egg
1 C. milk

2½ C. flour
2 tsp. baking powder
1 tsp. vanilla
Cinnamon-sugar mixture.

Combine sugar, butter and egg. Add milk, vanilla and dry ingredients. Place half of the batter in an 8×8-inch pan. Cover with a cinnamon-sugar mixture. Spread remaining batter over the first layer and top with more cinnamon and sugar. Bake at 350° for 20 minutes.

Zucchini Bread

3 eggs
1 C. oil
2 C. sugar
2 C. grated and peeled zucchini
3 tsp. vanilla

3 C. flour
1 tsp. salt
1 tsp. baking soda
3 tsp. cinnamon
¼ tsp. baking powder

Beat eggs until foamy; add next 4 ingredients. Mix lightly, but well. Add sifted dry ingredients, mix until blended. Divide into 2 greased loaf pans. Bake at 325° for 1 hour. Remove and cool on rack. Will freeze well.

One Hour Zucchini Bread

1 C. white sugar
1 C. brown sugar
3 eggs
½ C. vegetable oil
2 tsp. vanilla
3 C. flour

1 tsp. soda
½ tsp. baking powder
½ tsp. salt
2 tsp. cinnamon
2 C. zucchini (peeled and grated)

Put in 3 medium loaf pans. Bake at 325° for 60 minutes.

Dang Good Cake

1 C. brown sugar
1¼ C. water
2 tsp. cinnamon
½ C. lard

2 C. raisins
½ tsp. nutmeg
¼ tsp. cloves

Mix and boil for 3 minutes. Cool. Mix and dissolve 1 tsp. salt and 1 tsp. soda, 2 tsp. water. Add to other mixture plus 2 C. flour and 1 tsp. baking powder. Bake 50 minutes at 325°. Use greased and floured 9 × 13-inch cake pan. Eat as is or frost with powdered sugar frosting.

German Cheese Cake

4 C. pot cheese
4 eggs
1 C. sugar
¼ C. melted butter

1 C. light cream or rich milk
1 T. cornstarch
1 T. vanilla
1 tsp. salt

Put cheese through a strainer and beat eggs until light. Then combine all ingredients. Use rich biscuit dough for bottom crust. Fill with mixtures and sprinkle with cinnamon. Bake at 450° for 15 minutes and then at 375° for 1 hour.

"Just For Notes"

DESSERTS

HOME MADE
PIES
A SPECIALTY

Desserts

Dessert - Continued

"Just For Notes"

Pie Crust

3 C. flour
1 tsp. salt
1 C. lard

1 egg (slightly beaten)
½ tsp. vinegar
5 T. ice water

Cut lard into flour and salt until particles are the size of peas. Mix in the egg, vinegar and ice water. Gather pastry into a bowl and roll out on floured pastry sheet. Makes 2 double crust pies.

Apple Pie

6 C. sliced tart juicy apples
¾ C. sugar

¾ tsp. cinnamon
1 T. butter

Preheat oven to 425°. Combine apples, sugar and spice. Heap into pastry lined pie pan; dot with butter. Cover with top crust. Seal and flute edges. Bake at 425° for 50-60 minutes until done.

Squash Pie

2 eggs (separated)
2 C. cooked squash
1 C. cream
½ C. sugar
2 T. sugar

1/8 tsp. salt
½ tsp. cinnamon
½ tsp. allspice
½ tsp. lemon extract
Unbaked pie crust

Combine egg yolks, squash, cream and ½ C. sugar; mix well and place in a saucepan. Stir and cook to a custard. Remove from heat; add salt, spices and extract. Mix well and pour into pie crust. Bake 45-50 minutes at 425°. Top with meringue made by beating egg white with 2 T. sugar. Bake 15 minutes until top is light brown.

Sweet Potato Pie

1 C. sugar
1 C. milk
3 eggs (separated)
Unbaked pie crust

2 C. sweet potatoes (cooked & mashed)
2 tsp. cinnamon
3 T. sugar

To sweet potatoes, add 1 C. sugar, milk, cinnamon and beaten egg yolks. Pour into pie crust; bake for 60 minutes in a moderate oven. Make meringue of egg whites beaten stiff with 3 T. sugar. Spread meringue over pie; brown slightly in oven.

Molasses Pie

½ C. molasses
1½ C. milk
3 eggs
2 T. sugar

¼ tsp. cinnamon
¼ tsp. nutmeg
½ tsp. salt
Unbaked pie crust

Separate 2 of eggs (save whites for meringue); then beat the two yolks with the remaining egg. Scald milk, then pour over eggs; stir well. Add molasses salt and spice. Allow to cool; pour into pie crust. Bake at 400° for 10 minutes,then lower heat to 350°. Bake until knife comes clean. Beat sugar with remaining egg whites until stiff, cover pie with this meringue. Place back in oven, brown in moderate heat.

Pumpkin Pie

1½ C. pumpkin (canned)
⅔ C. brown sugar
2 C. milk
Unbaked pie crust (large)

2 beaten eggs
1 tsp. cinnamon
½ tsp. ginger
1 tsp. salt

Mix together pumpkin, sugar and milk. Mix in eggs, spices and salt; pour into pie crust. Bake at 450° for 10 minutes, then at 325° until tests done. Whipped cream is very good for topping.

Rhubarb Pie

4 C. chopped rhubarb
1¼ C. sugar
¼ C. orange juice
2 T. butter

3 T. butter
1 grated orange rind
¼ tsp. salt
Unbaked pie crust, pastry

Combine rhubarb, sugar, flour and salt; mix well. Mix in orange juice and rind. Pour into pie crust; spot with butter. Lattice pastry on top. Bake at 450° for about 20 minutes, then reduce to 350° and bake for another 20 minutes.

Apfel Kuchen

1 C. milk
2 C. sifted flour
1 well beaten egg
3 apples (pared and quartered)
Brown sugar

2 tsp. baking powder
1 T. shortening (melted)
½ tsp. salt
Cinnamon

Butter a shallow pan. Mix well together milk, egg, shortening, salt and baking powder. Add flour, mix well and pour into pan. Press apple pieces into top of batter, sprinkle with brown sugar liberally and a little cinnamon. Bake 30-35 minutes in a moderate oven.

Green Apple Pie

Any chance you have to get some green apples, try this recipe. I think you will enjoy it.

4 C. green apples (peeled & sliced)	*¼ tsp. nutmeg*
1 C. sugar	*Lemon juice (few drops)*
½ tsp. cinnamon	*Butter*

Place peeled and sliced green apples in unbaked pie shell. Add sugar, nutmeg, a few drop of lemon juice and a few dabs of butter. Place unbaked top crust on and bake in moderate oven.

Apple Dumplin's

Make a rich biscuit dough, the same as soda or baking powder biscuit, only adding a little more shortening. Take a pices of dough out on the molding-board, roll out almost as thin as pie crust; then cut into square pieces large enough to cover an apple. Put into the middle of each piece two apple halves that have been pared and cored; sprinkle on a spoonful of sugar and a pinch of ground cinnamon, turn the ends of the dough over the apple and lap them tight.

Lay dumplings in a dripping pan (buttered), the smooth side upward. When the pans are filled, put a small piece of butter on top of each, sprinkle over a large handful of sugar, turn in a cup of boiling water, then place in a moderate oven for three-quarters of an hour. Baste with brandy once while baking. Serve with pudding, sauce or cream and sugar.

Early Day Puddin'

6 T. corn meal
1 qt. milk
½ pt. cold water
½ C. suet chopped
2 level tsp. salt
3 T. brown sugar

1 C. molasses
1 level tsp. soda
1 T. ginger
½ tsp. cinnamon
⅓ tsp. nutmeg
4 eggs

Put the milk on to boil, wet the corn meal iwth the cold water and as soon as it boils stir in the corn meal, slt and suet, boil 15 minutes, stirring all the time. Chop the suet very fine, taking all the skin off. Take it off of the fire, put in ½ C. of cold milk, the sugar, molasses; stir the soda into the molasses; add the spices, beat the yolks well and beat in last the stiff beaten whites. Butter a two-quart pan and bake immediately for over 1 hour. When done there will be whey in the center. Let cool a little and serve with cream.

Old Fashioned Custard Pie

3 large eggs
½ C. sugar
½ tsp. salt

½ tsp. nutmeg
2⅔ C. milk
Unbaked pie shell

Beat eggs slightly, then add sugar, salt, nutmeg and milk. Beat well together and pour into unbaked pie shell, then bake 40 minutes in moderate oven. Sprinkle with fresh ground nutmeg.

Corn Meal Puddin'

1 pt. sorghum molasses	1 tsp. pulverized cinnamon
1 pt. milk	1 tsp. nutmeg
4 eggs	1 tsp. baking soda
1 C. beef suet chopped fine	1 tsp. salt
(or ½ C. butter)	Corn meal

Warm sorghum molasses and milk, stir well together. Beat eggs and stir gradually into molasses and milk; add beef suet (or butter) and corn meal sufficient to make a thick batter. Add cinnamon, nutmeg, soda and salt. Stir all together thoroughly. Dip a cloth into boiling water, shake, flour a little and turn in the mixture. Tie up, (leaving room for the pudding ot swell) and boil 3 hours. Serve hot with sauce made of drawn butter, wine and nutmeg.

Tarts

¾ C. shortening	1½ C. sugar
2 eggs	1 tsp. vanilla
1 T. milk	4 tsp. baking powder
3 C. flour	½ tsp. salt

Cream together sugar and shortening and beat in eggs. Add remaining ingredients and mix well. Roll out very thin on floured board. Cut out and bake 8 minutes at 350°. Makes a rich, crisp cookie. Mighty good!

Chocolate Bread Puddin'

We shore liked bread puddin', but had an' awful lot of trouble gettin' stale bread crumbs. We was always so durned hongry-we didn't leave much bread to git stale.

1 C. stale bread crumbs	⅓ C. sugar
2 C. hot milk	1 egg
1 ounce chocolate	1/8 tsp. salt
½ tsp. vanilla	

Soak bread in milk 30 minutes; melt chocolate in saucepan placed over hot water; add ½ the sugar and enough milk taken from bread and milk to make of the consistency to pour; add to mixture with remaining sugar, eggs slightly beaten, salt and vanilla. Turn into a buttered dish and bake ¾ hour in moderate oven. Serve either hot or cold with cream.

Punkin Pie

You'll notice thet canned punkin is used in this recipe-thets fer them people whose punkin crop was porely this year.

3 T. flour	1 C. condensed milk
½ tsp. cinnamon	2 eggs
½ tsp. nutmeg	¾ C. sugar
2 C. canned pumpkin	½ tsp. salt

Separate eggs and combine yolks with all other ingredients in iron skillet. Cook over moderate heat until thickened; set off to cool. Beat the egg whites to stiff peaks and then fold into the batch after it has cooled to a lukewarm temperature. Pour into baked pie shell. Serve with whipped cream or plain.

Bachelors Pie

1½ C. cooked beef   ¾ C. cooked carrot (diced)
  (cut up in hunks)   ½ C. celery (cut up)
2 C. milk   ½ chopped green pepper
4 T. flour   Mahed potaotes
⅓ chopped onion   Seasonings

Combine onion, celery, beef and pepper in big skillet with a little cooking fat in it. Brown slowly and stir constantly. When browned add the rest of the ingredients, stir till pretty hot again and pour into a greased baking dish. Then on top spread some mashed potatoes. Bake at 300° until brown.

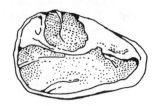

Blackberry Pie

4 C. blackberries   1/8 tsp. salt
1½ C. sugar   1½ T. butter
2 T. flour   Unbaked pie crust, pastry

Combine blackberries, sugar, salt and flour. Pour into pie crust; spot butter around on top. Lattice with pastry for top crust. Bake at 450° for 10 minutes, then for 30 minutes at 350° until crust is brown.

Sorghum Molasses Pie

2 C. molasses   1 T. melted butter
1 C. sugar   Juice of 1 lemon
3 eggs   Pinch of nutmeg

Combine all ingredients in mixing bowl and beat well. Pour into pastry and bake in moderate oven until done.

Gooseberry Pie

2 C. gooseberries   2 C. sugar

Add 1 T. of flour if berries are real juicy.

Mix berries and sugar in bowl and pour into unbaked pie shell. Add top crust that is slit to let out the steam. Bake in 425° oven for about 35 minutes, or until golden brown.

Jelly Roll

1 C. flour   1 C. sugar
1 tsp. salt (scant)   ⅓ C. boiling water
1½ tsp. baking powder   1 glass jelly
2 eggs (well beaten)   Powdered sugar

Beat sugar and eggs together. Sift flour, baking powder, salt together and add to mixture. Ad hot water last and mix well. Bake in buttered pan (shallow) for about 20-25 minutes in 375° oven. Turn out on a damp cloth, trim off hard edges, spread with jelly and roll quickly. Sprinkle with powdered sugar. Wrap in wax paper to hold till set; and when set, serve.

Vinegar Pie

1 C. sugar
2 eggs
2 T. vinegar
2 T. flour (or corn starch)

1 C. water
Small lump butter or margarine
½ tsp. lemon extract

Combine sugar, eggs, vinegar, flour (or corn starch) and water in double boiler and cook until thick and smooth, stirring occasionally. Just before removing from heat stir in small lump of butter and some lemon extract. Pour into baked pie shell. If desired, the pie may be topped with frosting or whipped cream.

Rhubarb Pie

Rhubarb
Nutmeg
Flour

Butter
1 C. sugar
⅓ C. molasses

Wash the stalks of rhubarb and strip off the thin stringy skin. Cut up in ½-inch pieces. Line a deep pie plate with unbaked pastry and fill it nearly full of rhubarb. Sprinkle some nutmeg on it, sift a little flour, put bits of butter on, 1 C. of sugar and ⅓ C. molasses. Do not use any water as the rhubarb is juicy. Place top crust on and bake in moderate oven till done.

Peanut Butter Pie

1 baked 9-inch pie shell.

BOTTOM LAYER:
1 C. powdered sugar   *⅓ C. creamy peanut butter*

FILLING:
¼ C. cornstarch   *2 C. scalded milk*
⅔ C. sugar   *3 egg yolks (beaten)*
¼ tsp. salt   *¼ tsp. vanilla*

TOPPING:
3 egg whites (beaten)

For Bottom Layer: Mix powdered sugar and peanut butter until like cornmeal. Spread ½ of this mixture in bottom of baked pie shell.

For Filling: Combine cornstarch, sugar, salt, scalded milk and beaten egg yolks. Cook until thick. Add vanilla and spread over peanut butter layer in pie crust.

For Topping: Beat egg white. Spread over pie filling and sprinkle with rest of peanut butter mixture over egg whites. Bake until light brown, 20 minutes.

Baked Apples

Use any good baking apple. Cut in half and core, but do not peel. Place in deep baking pan or dish. Pour some water around apples. Put on each apple; 2 T. of brown sugar and 1 tsp. of butter. Bake at 360 until done and tender. Baste once in a white.

Green Corn Puddin'

Take 12 ears or green corn; scrape the substance out with a spoon. Add yolks and whites, beaten separately, of 4 large eggs, 1 tsp. sugar, the same of flour rubbed into a tablespoon of butter, salt and pepper (to taste) and a pint of milk. Bake 45 minutes at 325°.

Maw's Paw Paw Pie

1 C. sugar
1 C. milk
1 egg

¼ tsp. salt
1½ C. paw paws (peeled &
  seeded)

Place all ingredients into stew pan and stir together. Cook over medium heat until thickened. Pour into unbaked pie shell and bake until the crust is done. Can be topped with meringue or other topping.

Apple Puddin'

1 egg
¾ C. sugar
2 T. flour
1¼ tsp. baking powder

1/8 tsp. salt
1 C. chopped nuts
½ C. chopped apples
1 tsp. vanilla

Beat egg and sugar together until smooth, combine flour, baking powder, salt; stir into egg mixture. Add nuts, apples and vanilla. Bake in a greased pie pan in moderate oven (325°) for 30 minutes. Serve with whipped cream or ice cream.

Apple Oatmeal Pudding

3 C. sliced apples
½ C. sugar
1 T. flour
1/8 tsp. salt
1/8 tsp. cinnamon
½ C. brown sugar

½ C. flour
½ C. raw oatmeal
1/8 tsp. salt
1/8 tsp. baking powder
¼ C. butter

Combine sliced apples, sugar, flour, salt and cinnamon. Place in baking dish. Crumble with fingers the brown sugar, flour, oatmeal, salt, baking powder and butter. Put on top of first layer and bake at 350° for 30-40 minutes or until apples are tender.

Cream Puffs

½ C. butter or oleo
1 C. boiling water
1 C. sifted all-purpose flour

¼ tsp. salt
4 eggs

Time: 40 minutes. Temperature: 400° for 15 minutes, 325° for 25 minutes. Melt butter in boiling water. Add flour and salt all at one time. Stir vigorously. Cook, stirring constantly, until the mixture forms a ball that doesn't separate. Comes away from sides of the pan. Remove from heat and cool slightly. Add eggs one at a time, beating hard after each addition until mixture is smooth. Can put them through a press or drop on greased cooking sheet, 2½-inches in size, 2-inches apart. Bake. Remove from cookie sheet and cool on a wire rack. When cold, cut hole in side and cut in half and fill with custard or whipped cream.

Peanut Butter Pie

1 C. corn syrup
1 C. sugar
½ tsp. vanilla

3 eggs (slightly beaten)
⅓ C. creamy peanut butter
Unbaked pie shell

Blend filling ingredients. Pour into unbaked pie shell. Bake at 400° for 15 minutes. Reduce heat to 350° and bake 30-35 minutes longer. Filling should appear slightly less set in center than around edges.

Elderberry Pie

2 C. sugar
1 pt. berries
1 pt. water
3 T. flour

Juice of ½ lemon
¼ tsp. cinnamon
Dash salt
Unbaked pastry for 2 crust pie

Combine in bowl the berries, lemon juice and water. Then add: sugar, salt, flour and cinnamon and mix well. Pour into rich unbaked pie shell and place unbaked crust on top. Bake about 425° for about 35 minutes.

Apple Dumplings
(Real Good)

1½ C. sugar
1½ C. water
¼ tsp. cinnamon
½ tsp. nutmeg
3 T. butter or oleo
6 medium (any good) cooking apples

2 C. flour
2 tsp. baking powder
1 tsp. salt
⅔ C. shortening
½ C. milk

Combine sugar, water, spices. Bring to a boil; add butter. Sift together dry ingredients and cut in shortening. Add milk all at once and stir until flour is just moistened. Roll 1/8-inch thick on a floured surface. Cut with a knife into squares. Place the apple halves together after putting a pinch of butter, sugar, nutmeg and cinnamon where the core was. Then wrap the dough firmly around apple. (I use both hads to press it around.) Place apples about 1-inch apart in a baking dish. Prick the top with sunburst pattern and pour the syrup over the apples. Have the oven hot before you put them in because the syrup causes them to soften up too much and come apart. Heat oven to 375° about 35 minutes.

Clara's Rhubarb Torte

3 C. diced rhubarb
1 C. sifted flour
1 C. sugar
¾ T. salt

1 unbeaten egg
½ C. shortening
1 tsp. baking powder

Place rhubarb in square pan. Put ½ C. sugar over rhubarb. Mix flour, ½ C. sugar, salt, egg, shortening and baking powder; sprinkle over rhubarb. Bake in moderate oven.

Rhubarb Dessert

1½ C. flour
7 T. powdered sugar
¾ C. oleo
2½ C. sugar
¼ C. flour

1 tsp. vanilla
3 beaten eggs
Dash of salt
1 C. evaporated milk

Crumb flour, powder sugar and oleo; pat in ungreased 9 × 13-inch pan. Bake at 325° for 15 minutes. Sprinkle 4 C. or more rhubarb on hot crust. Then pour over the rest of the ingredients. Bake at 325° for 45-60 minutes.

Peach Upside Down Cake

1 C. brown sugar
½ C. Crisco
1 C. white sugar
½ C. Crisco
1 egg
½ C. milk

1½ C. flour
2 tsp. baking powder
¼ tsp. salt
1 tsp. vanilla
Peaches

Place brown sugar and Crisco in large iron skillet. When melted, place in pan as many sliced or halved peaches as possible. Pour the cake mixture over peaches. Bake at 350° for 40 minutes. Turn out on cake plate, peach side up. May be served with whipped cream.

Rhubarb Crisp

4 C. cut rhubarb
1¼ C. sugar
½ tsp. cinnamon
1 T. flour
¾ C. flour

½ C. oatmeal
½ C. packed brown sugar
½ C. margarine
Salt

Place rhubarb in shallow pan. Combine sugar, flour and cinnamon. Sprinkle over fruit. For Topping: Mix ¾ C. flour, brown sugar and a dash of salt. Cut in margarine and stir in oatmeal. Sprinkle over fruit and bake at 350° for 1 hour. Makes 8 servings. 345 calories.

Rhubarb Dessert

Rhubarb
1½ C. sugar
2 (3 oz. ea.) boxes Jello
  (strawberry, raspberry or cherry)

1½ C. flour
½ C. powdered sugar
¾ C. butter

In a 9×13-inch pan, cut up rhubarb to fill the pan ¾ full. Mix the sugar and Jello together and mix in the rhubarb well. Mix the flour, powdered sugar and butter until crumbly, then sprinkle on top of the rhubarb mixture, evenly. Bake at 350° for 30 minutes. Serve with Cool Whip or other whipped topping.

Fried Apple Pies

Make a nice rich pastry dough. Cut in 5 or 6 inch squares. Place some cooked apples in and fold over. Moisten edgees to make them stick together. Fry in deep fat at about 370° until done. They will be puffed and brown when done. Drain on paper towels to get rid of grease.

Fruit Cobbler

1 C. sugar	2 tsp. baking powder
1 T. butter	2 C. fruit
1 egg	2 C. boiling water or juice
1 C. milk	1 C. sugar
2 C. flour	

Combine sugar, butter, egg, milk, flour and baking powder. Pour in a 9 x 13-inch pan. Mix together fruit, boiling water and sugar. Pour over first layer. Bake at 350° for 30 minutes. Rhubarb is a delicious fruit to use, but any kind of fruit is good.

Frozen Lemon Dessert

12 graham crackers	Juice and grated rind of 1 lemon
(1⅓ C. crushed)	1 C. whipping cream
2 T. sugar	½ C. sugar
¼ C. butter	3 eggs (separated)

For Crumb Crust: Mix graham crackers, 2 T. sugar and butter. Put in refrigerator to set and chill while mixing filling.

For Filling: Beat egg yolks. Add lemon and sugar, beaten egg whites and fold in whipped cream. Put in graham cracker crust. Save a few crumbs to sprinkle on top. Freeze. You can use a pie pan or a square pan.

Chocolate Lush

2 T. margarine
½ C. sugar
1 tsp. vanilla
1 C. all-purpose flour
3 T. cocoa
1 tsp. baking powder
½ tsp. salt

½ C. milk
½ C. nuts
1⅔ C. boiling water
½ C. sugar
5 T. cocoa
¼ tsp. salt

Melt margarine; add sugar and vanilla. Mix flour, 3 T. cocoa, baking poowder and salt. Stir into first mixture alternately with milk. Add nuts. Put in an 8×8×2-inch glass dish. Pour the mixture of boiling water, sugar, cocoa and salt over top. Bake at 350° for 25 minutes. Can be baked in microwave for about 8 minutes. Turn once during baking. If you desire a more moist pudding use 2 C. boiling water instead of 1⅔ C. Serve with your favorite sauce, whipped cream or ice cream.

Custard

Heat 1 quart milk. Add ⅔ C. sugar, 1/8 tsp. salt and 1 tsp. vanilla. Beat 6 eggs. Stir hot milk mixture into eggs. Pour into buttered dish. Sprinkle cinnamon on top. Bake in slow 325° oven, until knife inserted into center comes out clean. (If you use custard cups, this will make 10.)

Apple Dumplings

SYRUP:
2 C. sugar
2 C. water
¼ tsp. cinnamon

¼ tsp. nutmeg
¼ C. butter or margarine

DOUGH:
2 C. flour
1 tsp. salt
2 tsp. baking powder

¾ C. shortening
½ C. milk

Make syrup of sugar, water, cinnamon and nutmeg; add butter. Pare and core apples, cut into fourths. Sift flour, salt and baking powder. Cut in shortening. Add milk all at once and stir until moistened. Roll ¼-inch thick, cut into 5-inch squares. Arrange 4 pieces of apple on each square, sprinkle generously with additional sugar, cinnamon and nutmeg, dot with butter. Fold corners to center, pinch edges together. Place 1-inch apart in greased baking pan about 9 × 13-inch pan. Pour syrup over them. Bake in moderate oven 375°, about 35 minutes. Makes 8 dumplings.

Bread Pudding

2¼ C. milk
2 slightly beaten eggs
2 C. (1-inch) day old bread cubes
½ C. brown sugar

½ tsp. cinnamon
1 tsp. vanilla
¼ tsp. salt
½ C. seedless raisins (opt.)

Combine milk and eggs, pour over bread cubes. Stir in rmaining ingredients. Bake at 350° about 45 minutes or until a knife comes out clean. Top with whipped cream or ice cream.

Baked Custard

3 eggs (slightly beaten)
2 T. sugar
¼ tsp. salt
1/8 tsp. nutmeg

2 C. skim milk
½ tsp. vanilla
Dash cinnamon

Preheat oven to 325°. Combine eggs, sugar, salt and nutmeg. Slowly stir in milk and vanilla. Set 6 (5 oz. each) custard cups in shallow pan. Pour hot water in pan to level of about 1-inch. Pour custard into cups. Sprinkle with cinnamon. Bake for 40 minutes or until knife inserted in custard comes out clean.

Bread Pudding

¾ C. brown sugar
¾ C. raisins
3 slices buttered bread cubes (dry)

2 C. milk
1 tsp. vanilla
2 eggs

Put brown sugar and raisins in double boiler. Then put in bread cubes. Mix milk, eggs and vanilla together well. Then pour over bread cubes and steam 1 hour. Don't stir. The sugar and raisins are to stay in bottom of boiler when cooking.

Mom's Apple Crisp Pudding

6 or 8 apples (sliced)
1 tsp. cinnamon
½ C. water

½ C. butter
1 C. sugar
¾ C. flour

Butter casserole and add apples, water and cinnamon. Work together sugar, flour and butter until crumbly; sprinkle over apple mixture. Bake, uncovered at 350° for 30 minutes.

Blackberry Puddin'

Sounds kind'a good, don't it? Try it, it's real good.

2 C. sugar
2 C. flour (sifted)
⅓ C. butter
2 C. boiling water

1 tsp. salt
2 tsp. baking powder
1 C. milk
2 C. blackberries

Cream 1 C. sugar and the butter together. Add the flour, baking powder, salt, milk and mix well. Then pour blackberries on top and then pour 1 C. sugar and the 2 C. of boiling water. Bake in moderate oven 350°, until top is golden brown. Will take about 50 minutes.

Tapioca Pudding

3 eggs (separated)
1 C. sugar
1 qt. milk

¼ C. tapioca (heaping)
1 tsp. vanilla

Mix and boil 3 egg yolks (beaten), sugar, milk and tapioca. Beat egg whites stiff and add to mixture. Remove from heat and add vanilla; stir well.

Peppermint Pie

1 env. unlfavored gelatin
¼ C. sugar
1/8 tsp. salt
2 eggs (separated)

1¼ C. milk
½ C. crushed peppermint stick
　candy
Few drops red food coloring
Whipped cream

Mix together gelatin, sugar and salt. Add 2 egg yolks and milk. Cook in double boiler, stirring until dissolved and slightly thickened. Remove from heat and stir in crushed peppermint stick and few drops red food coloring to light pink. Chill until slightly thicker than unbeaten egg whites. Beat egg whites until stiff; add ¼ C. sugar gradually. Fold into chilled mixture, then fold in 1 C. whipped cream. Pour into baked pie shell. Garnish with whipped cream (and then sprinkle lightly with crushed peppermint, if desired). A light dessert after a heavy meal.

Dessert Bread Pudding

¾ C. (or less) brown sugar
3 slices bread (cubed)
3 eggs (beaten)
1½ C. milk

½ tsp. vanilla
½ tsp. cinnamon
½ C. raisins

Put brown sugar in bottom of greased double boiler. Add bread cubes. Don't stir. Add raisins. Beat eggs with milk and pour over mixture. Do not stir or peek. Cook for 1 hour with lid on. Keep water boiling.

Baked Custard

6 eggs
¾ C. sugar
½ tsp. salt

4 C. scalded milk
½ tsp. vanilla
Nutmeg, as desired

Beat eggs; add sugar and salt, mixing well. Add milk, scalded or not and vanilla. Bake at 350°-375° for 1-1½ hours, depending on depth of baking dish. Place baking dish in larger pan that has 1-1½-inch hot water in it, to bake.

Orange Pudding

3 eggs
2 tsp. flour
1 C. sugar
1¼ C. water

1 tsp. lemon juice
3 oranges (cut up)
2 T. sugar

Beat egg yolks until fluffy. Sift in flour and sugar. Add water and boil until it thickens. Add lemon juice. Pour over cut-up oranges. Add beaten whites of eggs, sweetened with 2 T. sugar.

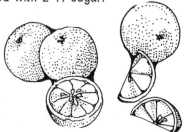

Poor Man's Cocoa Pudding
(No milk, No eggs)

1 C. sugar
4 T. flour (rounded)
4 T. cocoa (level)
½ tsp. salt

2½ C. boiling water
Margarine (size of walnut)
2 tsp. vanilla

Mix flour, cocoa, sugar and salt; add boiling water slowly and stir well. Cook until thick. Add vanilla and margarine.

Rhubarb Crisp

¾ C. sugar   1 egg
2 T. flour   3 C. diced rhubarb

Spread in 9×9-inch or 6×10-inch pan and top with:

4 T. butter   ⅔ C. flour
6 T. brown sugar

Bake at 375° for 30 minutes. (We usually double the recipe and use a 9×13-inch pan.)

Old Fashioned Bread Pudding

8 slices of bread (broken up)   3 eggs
1 C. sugar   1 qt. milk
1 C. raisins   1 tsp. salt

Combine all ingredients and put in cake pan. Bake at 350° for 45 minutes or knife inserted 1-inch from edge comes out clean.

Apple Crisp

6 apples (sliced)
1 C. sugar
1 T. cinnamon

2 C. brown sugar
1 C. flour
¼ C. butter

Mix apples, sugar and cinnamon; put in bottom of pie pan. Mix brown sugar, flour and butter. Put on top. Bake at 350° for 30-35 minutes. Let cool. Serve with whipped cream.

Peach Pie

2 C. peaches (peeled & sliced)
1/8 tsp. allspice
1 C. sugar

¼ C. water
1 tsp. butter
Unbaked pie crust & pastsry

Pour peaches in pie crust. Combine sugar and spice; sprinkle over peaches. Add water; dot with butter. Add top crust and stick with a fork to vent. Bake at 430° for about 40 minutes.

Pie Crust With Milk

1 C. flour
½ tsp. salt

¼ C. shortening or lard
2⅓ T. (about) cold milk

Makes one 8-inch or 9-inch crust.

Coconut Pie

1 (9-inch) unbaked pie crust
3 eggs
1 T. flour
¾ C. sugar

1 C. light corn syrup
2 T. margarine (melted)
1 tsp. vanilla
1½ C. coconut

Beat eggs, sugar and flour. Add syrup and melted margarine and beat. Add vanilla and beat. Sprinkle coconut over bottom of unbaked pie crust. Pour the mixture over the coconut. Bake in slow oven (325°) for 40-45 minutes or until firm.

Gooseberry Pie

4 C. green gooseberries
¾-1 C. sugar (depending on
    sourness of berries)

1½ T. flour
1/8 tsp. salt
1½ T. butter

Combine sugar, flour and salt. Sprinkle over berries, stirring to distribute. Turn into pie shell, dot with butter and brush edge of pastry with water. Cover with pastry and slash. Bake in 450° oven for 15 minutes or until crust is delicately browned. Reduce heat to 350° and continue baking 20-25 minutes or until berries are tender.

At Home Lemon Pudding

1 C. sugar
1 T. butter
1 lemon (juice & rind)

2 T. flour
2 eggs
1 C. milk

Cream 1 C. sugar with 1 T. butter. Add juice and rind of 1 lemon, 2 T. flour, yolks of 2 eggs, 1 C. milk and last add beaten whites of 2 eggs. Set in a pan of warm water until done, or for about 1 hour (350°) oven.

"Just For Notes"

BARS

N'

COOKIES

Bars And Cookies

Bars And Cookies - Continued

"Just For Notes"

Brownies

1½ C. sifted flour
8 T. cocoa
1 tsp. salt
2 C. sugar

1 C. softened margarine
4 unbeaten eggs
2 tsp. vanilla
1 C. nuts (opt.)

Preheat oven to 325°. Grease or spray with cooking spray, the bottom and sides of an oblong glass baking dish. Combine dry ingredients. Combine margarine, eggs and sugar. Mix. Add dry ingredients, vanilla and nuts. Mix. Batter will be thick. Pour into baking dish spreading evenly. Bake 30-35 minutes. Do Not Overbake. Frost with your favorite frosting or sprinkle with powdered sugar.

Graham Crax Bars

½ C. butter
1 C. brown sugar
1 C. crushed graham crackers

⅓ C. milk
1 C. flaked coconut

Cook 5 minutes, stir all the time. Spread between layers of graham crackers. Top with powdered sugar and cocoa frosting. Cut into bars.

Coconut Dream Bars

½ C. brown sugar (packed)   1 C. flour
½ C. butter

Blend like pie crust the first 3 ingredients and spread in 9×13-inch pan.
Bake 10 minutes at 325°.

1 C. brown sugar   1 tsp. vanilla
2 T. flour   1 C. coconut
½ tsp. baking powder   1 C. chopped nuts
2 eggs (beat well)   Salt (pinch

Mix remaining ingredients and spread over top of first mixture. Bake 20
minutes at 350°.

Lemon Crumb Squares

1 can sweetened milk   ½ tsp. salt
½ C. lemon juice   ⅔ C. butter
1 tsp. lemon peel   1 C. brown sugar
1½ C. flour   1 C. uncooked oatmeal
1 tsp. baking powder

Blend together condensed milk, juice and lemon peel. Set aside. Cream butter; add sugar and blend well. Add oatmeal. Sift flour, baking powder and
salt. Add to oatmeal mixture. Mix until crumbly. Put in pan. Spread. Save
some of crumb mixture. Spread lemon mixture on top. Cover with rest of
curmb mixture. Bake at 350° for 25 minutes, until brown around edges.
Cool in pan for 15 minutes. Cut into squares and chill in pan until firm.

Luscious Lemon Bar Cookies

CRUST:
1 C. soft oleo
Dash salt

½ C. powdered sugar
2 C. flour

Combine above and mix well. Press mixture into 9×13-inch pan. Bake 15 minutes at 350° or until lightly brown. Cool.

FILLING:
4 eggs (beaten)
2 C. sugar

¼ C. flour
6 T. lemon juice

Combine eggs (beat well), flour, sugar and lemon juice. Pour into crust. Bake at 350° for 25 minutes or until set. Cool and sprinkle with powdered sugar. Makes 3 dozen cookies.

Peanut Bars

3 eggs
1½ C. sugar
2 C. flour
1 C. cold water
2 tsp. baking powder

½ tsp. salt
1 tsp. vanilla
Ground peanuts
Powdered sugar

Beat eggs about 2 minutes. Add sugar and beat 5 minutes. Add 1 C. flour and beat well. Add water, baking powder and second cup of flour. Beat. Add salt and vanilla. Bake in moderate oven about 30 minutes. Springs back to touch when done. Cut into small bars. Make a thin milk and powdered sugar frosting (about the consistency of whipping cream). Dip each bar in the frosting and roll in ground nuts.

Yummy Bars

¾ C. white sugar
½ C. shortening
2 eggs
1 tsp. vanilla

¼ tsp. salt
2 T. cocoa
½ C. coconut
½ C. nuts (opt.)

TOPPING:
1 jar marshmallow creme
1 C. chocolate chips
1 C. butterscotch chips

1 C. peanut butter
1½ C. Rice Krispies

Cream together sugar, shortening, eggs and vanilla. Add remaining ingredients and beat well. Bake in a 9×13-inch cake pan 15-20 minutes at 350°. When cool, spread with marshmallow creme. Melt remaining ingredients together in double boiler. Add slightly crumbled Rice Krispies. Spread over bars and refrigerate.

Peanut Butter Chocolate Chip Cookies

1¼ C. flour
¾ tsp. baking soda
½ tsp. baking powder
¼ tsp. salt
¾ C. peanut butter
½ C. butter (softened; cna use
   Crisco butter)

½ C. sugar
½ C. brown sugar
½ tsp. vanilla
5 T. milk
1 egg
1 C. chocolate chips
½ C. chopped nuts

Combine flour, baking soda and powder in large bowl. Cream together peanut butter, butter, sugar, brown sugar in large bowl. Beat in milk, egg and vanilla. Add flour mixture. Then add chips and nuts. Bake at 350° for 10-12 minutes or until golden brown.

Joyce's Yummy Bars

14 oz. pkg. caramels
1/3 C. evaporated milk
1 box German chocolate cake mix
1 C. chopped nuts
6 oz. pkg. chocolate chips

1/3 C. evaporated milk
1/2 tsp. burnt sugar flavor
1/2 tsp. butter flavor
3/4 C. melted margarine

In top of double boiler, combine caramels and 1/3 C. evaporated milk. Cook until melted (or decrease evaporated milk to 1/4 C. and melt in microwave). Set aside. Grease a 9 x 13-inch pan. In bowl, combine cake mix, melted margarine, 1/3 C. evaporated milk, flavorings and nuts. Stir by hand until well mixed. Spread half of dough over bottom of pan. Bake at 350° for 6 minutes. Remove from oven. Sprinkle chocolate chips over baked crust. Spread caramel mixture over chocolate chips, and then carefully spread reserved dough over caramel layer. Bake 20 minutes. Cool slightly and cut into bars. These are rich and chewy.

Jiffy Chewy Bars

1 pkg. Jiffy yellow cake mix
1 T. water
2 T. flour
1/4 C. chocolate chips
1 egg

1/4 C. brown sugar
1 T. oleo
1 T. corn syrup
1/4-1/2 C. nuts

Mix all together. Bake in 8 x 8-inch pan at 350° for 25-30 minutes.

Iced Apple Brownies

3 eggs
1¾ C. sugar
1 C. oil
1 tsp. cinnamon
1 C. chopped nuts

2 C. flour
1 tsp. salt
1 tsp. baking soda
1 C. finely chopped apples

Cream eggs with sugar and oil. Add cinnamon and nuts. Stir in dry ingredients and apples. Pour into a 9×13-inch pan (greased) and bake in 350° preheated oven for 35-40 minutes.

ICING:
¼ C. butter
1 (3 oz.) pkg. cream cheese
  (softened)

1 C. nuts (finely chopped)
½ box (8 oz.) powdered sugar
1 tsp. vanilla

Beat all ingredients with mixer until smooth. Spread on cooled brownies.

Chocolate Syrup Brownies

1 stick oleo
4 eggs
1 tsp. vanilla

1 C. sugar
1 C. flour
1 can Hershey's syrup

Cream oleo and sugar; add eggs, chocolate syrup and mix well. Add vanilla, then flour. Put into greased cookie sheet pan. Bake at 350° for 20 minutes.

GOOD FROSTING:
6 T. oleo
1 C. sugar

6 T. milk

Bring to boil and boil for 1 minute. Remove. Add 1 C. chocolate chips and 1 tsp. vanilla.

Pumpkin Crunch Squares

16 oz. can pumpkin
13 oz. can evaporated milk
1 C. sugar
¼ tsp. salt
2 T. pumpkin spice

3 eggs
1 pkg. cake mix (spice is good)
¾ C. margarine (sliced)
1 C. chopped nuts

Mix the first 6 ingredients. Pour into an ungreased 9×13-inch pan. Sprinkle dry cake mix over the top. Dot with margarine and sprinkle on nuts. Bake at 350° for 55-60 minutes. Cool. Good served with whipped cream or ice cream.

Really Great Cookie Bars

½ C. margarine or butter
1½ C. graham cracker crumbs
1 can sweetened condensed milk
1 (6 oz.) pkg. semi-sweet chocolate chips

1 C. flaked coconut
1 C. chopped nuts
6 Hershey bars for topping

Preheat oven to 350° (325° for glass dish). Use 9×13-inch baking dish. Melt margarine in the dish. Sprinkle crumbs over margarine evenly. Pour sweetened condensed milk evenly over crumbs. Top with remaining ingredients; press down. Bake 25-30 minutes until evenly browned. Place bars on top. Melt and spread evenly. Cool.

Sleepy-Time Lemon Bar

1 pkg. one-step angel food cake mix *Powdered sugar icing*
1 (21 oz.) can lemon pie filling *Lemon extract flavoring*

With a spoon, stir together cake mix and pie filling. Do not use an electric mixer. Pour into ungreased jelly roll pan, 10½ × 15½-inches and bake in 350° oven for 20-25 minutes. When cool, frost with a powdered sugar frosting flavored with lemon extract.

Time-For-Friends Cookies

6 C. flour   *2 C. butter*
4 tsp. cream of tartar   *4 eggs*
2 tsp. soda   *3½ C. sugar*
1 tsp. salt   *2 tsp. vanilla*
                                 Anise flavoring (opt.)

Cream together butter and sugar. Add eggs and vanilla. Mix well. Add dry ingredients a little at a time, mixing well until all is added. Roll dough into quarter size balls and flatten with glass dipped in sugar. Makes a large batch. Bake until golden brown, 8-12 minutes at 350°.

Fudge Nut Bars

1 (6 oz.) pkg. chocolate chips	1 can Eagle Brand condensed milk
3 T. butter	¾ C. nuts
2 tsp. vanilla	1 C. shortening
2 C. brown sugar	1 tsp. soda
2 eggs	1 tsp. salt
1 tsp. vanilla	2½ C. quick oatmeal
2½ C. flour	

Melt chocolate chips and butter and milk, nuts and vanilla. Cream together other ingredients. Add oatmeal. Press ⅔ of cookie mixture in pan (greased 10 × 16-inch). Spread on fudge mixture. Then dab and spread rest of cookie mix on top. Bake at 350° for 20-25 minutes. Don't overbake.

Unbaked Caramel Cookies

2 C. sugar	4 oz. pkg. instant pudding
¾ C. oleo	(butterscotch or chocolate)
⅔ C. evaporated milk	3½ C. raw oatmeal

In large saucepan combine sugar, oleo, milk. Bring to boil for 5 mintues. Remove from heat; add pudding mix and oatmeal. Cool slightly. Drop by teaspoon on waxed paper. Let set until firm. Store in refrigerator. 1 C. coconut may also be added or nuts.

Peanut Butter Cookies

1½ C. sifted all-purpose flour	½ tsp. grated fresh orange
1½ tsp. baking powder	1½ tsp. pure vanilla
½ tsp. salt	1 egg (well beaten)
¼ C. margarine	⅓ C. orange juice
½ C. creamy peanut butter	Artificial sweetener to substitute for
	24 tsp. sugar

Preheat oven to 400°. Sift together flour, baking powder and salt. Cream together margarine, peanut butter, orange rind and vanilla. Add egg, orange juice and artificial sweetener; blend well. Add dry ingredients gradually; mix well after each addition. Measure 1 T. (level) dough for each cookie. Roll between hands to form ball. Place 2-inches apart on ungreased cookie sheet; flatten with fork. Bake about 15 minutes. Store cookies in a tightly covered tin. These cookies have better flavor and texture 24 hours after baking. Yield: 24 cookies.

Coffee Cookies

1 C. sugar
2 C. flour (sifted)
1 C. shortening
½ tsp. cloves
¾-1 C. cold coffee
1 egg (beaten)

¾ C. chopped nuts
½ tsp. baking soda
¼ tsp. salt
1 tsp. baking powder
½ tsp. cinnamon

Combine and cream together the sugar and shortening, then add the beaten egg and mix well. Combine sifted flour with spices, salt, baking soda and baking powder and mix well. Add with coffee to rest of the batch. Then add rest of the ingredients and enough flour or water, if needed to make the right consistency for dropping. Drop on oiled cookie sheet. Bake at 400° for 15 minutes.

Peanut Butter Cookies

½ C. white sugar
½ C. brown sugar
1 C. shortening
1 egg (beaten)

¾ C. peanut butter
1½ C. sifted flour
1 tsp. soda
1 tsp. vanilla

Combine and cream together the sugar, brown suar, shortening and vanilla. Ad beaten egg and beat well; then mix in peanut butter. Sift flour and soda into batch and stir. Form into shape desired on ungreased cookie sheet. Bake in moderate heat till done.

Boiled Cookies

2 C. sugar
½ C. milk
1/8 lb. butter
3 T. cocoa

3 C. quick oats
½ C. peanut butter or coconut
1 tsp. vanilla
½-1 C. nuts (if desired)

Put sugar, milk, butter and cocoa into pan. Bring to boil until it forms soft ball. Remove from heat, add oatmeal, peanut butter, vanilla and nuts. Stir well and drop by teaspoon on wax paper. Let stand ½ hour until dry.

Tasty Large Cookies

2 C. sugar
1 C. shortening
2 eggs
1 C. sour milk (buttermilk)

2 tsp. vanilla
3½ C. flour
2 tsp. soda
½ tsp. salt

Mix together and drop by large spoonsful onto cookie sheet. Bake 15 minutes at 375°.

Lisa's Sugar Cookies

1¾ C. white sugar
1½ C. lard
2 eggs
1 C. sweet or sour milk
1 tsp. (level) baking powder

2 tsp. (rounded) baking powder
1 tsp. vanilla
1 tsp. lemon juice
Pinch of salt
5 C. (approx.) flour

Mix all ingredients together and use just enough flour to make a soft dough. May take more but only use enough to handle dough. Refrigerate for a few hours or overnight, roll out. Bake at 400°, but if cookies spread out use more flour.

Sugar Cookies

CREAM TOGETHER:
1 C. sugar
1 C. butter
Add 2 eggs

1 C. powdered sugar
1 C. oil

SIFT TOGETHER:
4½ C. flour
1 tsp. cream of tartar

1 tsp. baking soda
1 tsp. vanilla (last)

Refrigerate overnight. Roll in balls and roll in sugar and press with a fork. Bake.

Old Fashioned Peanut Butter Cookies

2½ C. unsifted flour
1 tsp. baking soda
1 C. margarine
1 C. brown sugar
1 tsp. vanilla

1 tsp. baking powder
¼ tsp. salt
1 C. peanut butter (creamy or
  chunky)
2 eggs

Mix first 4 ingredients; set aside. Beat margarine, peanut butter, then add sugar, eggs and vanilla. Add flour mixture, beat until well blended. Chill dough. Shape into 1-inch balls. Place on ungreased cookie sheet; flatten slightly. Bake in 350° oven 12 minutes or until lightly browned. Makes 6 dozen cookies.

Date Cookies

1 C. white sugar
1 C. brown sugar
1 C. shortening
3 eggs

¼ tsp. salt
1 tsp. soda
4 C. flour
1 tsp. vanilla

Boil 1 lb. chopped dates, ¾ C. sugar and 1 C. boiling water. Let cool. Add ½ C. nutmeats chopped. Cream sugar and shortening. Add well beaten eggs and mix well. Dissolve soda in 2 T. hot water and add to sugar, etc. Add vanilla. Put the salt in flour and sift into batter a little at a time. Mix well. Divide the cookie dough into 2 equal parts and roll each part into a rectangle shape ¼-inch thick. Spread the cooled date filling over the 2 rectangles. Roll up as a jelly roll. Place in pan and chill 3 hours or overnight. Slice in 3/8-inch slices. Bake at 350° for 20 minutes.

Old Fashioned Ice Box Cookies

½ C. butter
1 C. brown sugar
1 egg
½ tsp. soda
1¾ C. flour

1/8 tsp. salt
½ tsp. cinnamon
½ tsp. vanilla
½ C. black walnut meats

Cream butter and sugar and beat in egg. Sift dry ingredients and add to butter mixture with vanilla and nut meats. Shape dough into long roll about 2-inches in diameter. Chill it until hard. Slice into very thin slices. Bake slices on greased sheet in moderate oven for 5-10 minutes.

Honey Cookies

5 T. margarine
4 T. hot water
½ tsp. soda

1 tsp. vanilla
1¼ C. flour
Honey

In a cup put in 5 T. melted margarine or butter, add 4 T. hot water. Fill the cup with honey, pour in bowl, add soda, vanilla and flour. This will be a soft dough. Drop by teaspoonsful on greased cookie sheet. Bake until they spring back when finger is pressed on them. Bake at 350° about 10 minutes. Frost with your favorite icing. (Here is the one I use: Melt 2 T. margarine, add 2 T. hot water, 1 tsp. vanilla, add powdered sugar to spread. If frosting gets too thick, add more water.)

Sugar Cookies

1 C. butter
3 eggs
3 C. flour
½ tsp. vanilla

1½ C. sugar
1 tsp. soda and 1 T. warm water
½ tsp. salt

Cream butter and sugar. Add eggs, vanilla, salt and soda. Add in flour. Roll out dough.

For Frosting: 1 T. Karo syrup and 1 egg yolk adding vanilla, milk and powdered sugar to desired texture and taste.

Beat Sugar Cookies

1 C. powdered sugar
1 C. butter or margarine
2 eggs
1 tsp. salt
1 tsp. cream of tartar

1 C. granulated sugar
1 C. vegetable oil
1 tsp. vanilla
1 tsp. soda
4 C. flour

Cream sugars, butter and oil. Add eggs, mix until fluffy. Add dry ingredients, mix well. Roll dough into balls the size of walnuts. Place on ungreased cookie sheet and press with glass dipped in sugar. Bake at 350° for 10 minutes.

Drop Sugar Cookies

2 C. sugar
1 C. shortening
1 tsp. vanilla
½ C. milk

4 C. flour
½ tsp. salt
1 tsp. soda
1 tsp. baking powder

Cream shortening and sugar; add 2 beaten eggs. Then add milk, vanilla and dry ingredients. May add nuts. Drop by spoonfuls on greased cookie sheet. Bake in 350° oven for 8-10 minutes. This can be kept in refrigerator for several days, then rolled in ball and flattened with spoon or something with design on it. (I roll the balls in sugar.)

Sugar Cookies

1 C. oleo
1 C. Crisco
1 C. white sugar
1 C. powdered sugar

2 eggs
2 tsp. vanilla
4 C. flour
1 tsp. soda
1 tsp. cream of tartar

Cream oleo, Crisco, white sugar and powdered sugar (I usually sift mine). Add eggs and vanilla. Mix well. Pour in flour, soda and cream of tartar; mix well. Make into small balls. Place on greased cookie sheets. Flatten with glass dipped in sugar. Red and green sugar is nice for Christmas. Bake at 350° until edges turn golden brown (approximately 10-12 minutes).

Sugar Cookies

6 C. flour
2 C. sugar
3 tsp. baking powder
1 tsp. salt

2 C. butter or oleo
2 eggs (beaten)
½ C. light cream or milk
2 tsp. vanilla

In mixing bowl, stir together dry ingredients. Cut in butter until mixture looks like coarse crumbs. Add egg, cream and vanilla. Mix well. On ''lightly'' floured surface roll out dugh to ¼-inch thick. Cut with cookie cutter. Place on greased sheet. Bake at 400° for 7-8 minutes or until ''just'' starting to brown.

Sugar Cookies

1 C. oleo (not butter or shortening)
2 C. powdered sugar
½ tsp. soda

1 egg
2½ C. sifted flour
1 tsp. vanilla

Cream oleo, powdered sugar, and soda together until smooth. Add egg and beat until smooth. Mix in vanilla. Add flour and stir until smooth. Form into balls and smash with a glass dipped in sugar on an ungreased baking sheet or refrigerate 1 hour or more. Roll and cut with cookie cutters. Decorate with colored sugars if desired or frost after baking. Bake 8-10 minutes in a 350° oven. Watch closely as they brown easily.

Sugar Cookies

1 C. granulated sugar
1 C. powdered sugar
1 C. margarine
1 C. oil
2 eggs (well beaten)

2 tsp. vanilla
1 tsp. cream of tartar
1 tsp. soda
5¼ C. flour

Cream sugar with margarine. Add beaten eggs. Stir in oil and vanilla. Mix dry ingredients and blend in. Form into balls. Dip in granulated sugar and flatten with bottom of glass. Bake at 350° until lightly browned, 8-10 minutes.

No Bake Corn Flake Cookies

½ C. white Karo
½ C. white sugar
2 T. cocoa

½ C. peanut butter
3 C. corn flakes

Place Karo, sugar and cocoa in saucepan and bring to a boil. Then remove from heat. Stir in peanut butter and corn flakes. Drop on waxed paper to cool.

Aunt Lou's Sugar Cookies

¾ C. sugar
⅓ C. shortening
⅓ C. oil
1 T. milk
2 tsp. almond extract

1 egg
1½ C. flour
1½ tsp. baking powder
¼ tsp. salt
Sugar to sprinkle on top

Heat oven to 375°. In large bowl, cream together sugar, shortening, oil, milk, almond extract and egg. Cream until light and fluffy. Stir in dry ingredients and blend well. Spread evenly in ungreased 15 × 10-inch jelly roll pan. Sprinkle with sugar. Bake in 375° oven for 12 minutes - light brown. Cool 5 minutes and cut into squares or use your favorite cookie cutters.

Cake Mixture Cookies

Cake mix
⅓ C. oil

1 tsp. vanilla
2 eggs

Combine ½ of cake mix with other ingredients. Mix well. Add rest of mix. If you wish, add nut meats, raisins, chocolate bits or butterscotch bits. Drop by teaspoon on slightly greased cookie sheet. Bake in preheated 350° oven for 8 minutes for chewy; 10 minutes for crisp.

Ginger Cookies

2½ C. flour
½ tsp. salt
1 tsp. cinnamon
1 C. brown sugar
¼ C. molasses
¼ C. sugar

2 tsp. soda (baking)
3 tsp. ginger
¾ C. butter
1 egg
1 T. lemon rind or 2 tsp. lemon juice

Preheat oven to 350°. Mix flour, soda, salt, ginger and cinnamon in bowl. Cream butter, brown sugar and egg in another bowl until fluffy. Beat in molasses and lemon rind. Stir in dry ingredients, half at at time; blend well after each time. Roll level teaspoonfuls of dough between palms into palms into balls; roll in sugar. Place on ungreased cookie sheet. Bake for 10 minutes.

Oatmeal Cookies

2 C. quick cooking oats   1 tsp. salt
2 C. firmly packed brown sugar   1 C. salad oil
1 tsp. almond extract

Drop by teaspoonful 2-inches apart, on a greased cookie sheet. Bake at 325°
for 15 minute. Store in tight covered container.

Oatmeal Cookies

1 C. butter or margarine   1 tsp. soda dissolved in 2 tsp.
1 C. brown sugar   hot water
1 egg   1½ C. flour (sifted)
1 tsp. vanilla   2½ C. oatmeal

Cream the butter and sugar. Add the egg and vanilla. Beat well. Mix the
flour and oatmeal, stir into the creamed mixture along with the soda. Roll
into balls the size of walnuts and flatten on cookie sheets. Bake at 375°
for 15 minutes.

Chistmas Butter Cookies

1¾ C. flour
½ tsp. baking powder
⅔ C. butter

½ C. sugar
1 small egg (well beaten)
½ tsp. vanilla

Sift flour with baking powder. Cream butter well; add sugar and continue creaming until well mixed. Mix in the beaten egg. Add vanilla. Stir in sifted dry ingredients in 2 or 3 portions until dough is just smooth. Roll out to 1/8-inch thick on a floured surface and cut into desired shapes. Bake on ungreased cookie sheet in a moderately hot oven (400°) for 6-8 minutes or until delicately browned. Makes 3-4 dozen cookies.

Oatmeal Crispies

1 C. shortening
1 C. brown sugar
1 C. white sugar
2 eggs (well beaten)
1½ C. flour

1 tsp. vanilla
1 tsp. salt
1 tsp. soda
3 C. quick oatmeal
½ C. nuts

Mix in order. Bake at 350° for 10 minutes.

Candy Cane Cookies

Preheat oven to 375°. Mix together thoroughly.

1 C. shortening
1 C. sifted confectioner's sugar
1 egg

1 tsp. vanilla
1½ tsp. almond extract

Sift together and stir in 2½ C. sifted flour, 1 tsp. salt. Divide dough in tow halves. Blend into one half ½ tsp. red food coloring. Roll 1 tsp. each color dough into a stipe about 4-inches long. Place strips side by side; press together and twist like a rope. Place on ungreased cookie sheet. Curve top down to form cane handle. Bake 9 minutes until brown. Roll in mixture of ½ C. sugar, ½ C. crushed peppermint candy.

Sugar Cookies

1 C. magarine
1 C. salad oil
2 C. sugar
2 eggs
½ tsp. salt

2 tsp. vanilla
5 C. flour
2 tsp. soda
2 tsp. cream of tartar

Mix togther and chill. Make walnut-size balls and flatten with bottom of glass dipped in sugar. Bake 10 minutes at 350°.

Orange Slice Cookies

1½ C. brown sugar
½ C. shortening
2 eggs
2 C. flour
1 tsp. soda

½ tsp. salt
1 lb. orange slice candy
½ C. flaked coconut or nuts
½ C. quick oatmeal

Cream sugar and shortening. Beat in eggs. Sift 1½ C. flour, soda and salt. Blend into creamed mixture. Cut orange slices into small pieces and mix with remaining ½ C. flour. Add with remaining ingredients. Drop by teaspoon onto greased cookie sheet. Bake at 325° for 10-12 minutes. Yields: 5 dozen.

"Just For Notes"

CANDY

Candy

Gumdrop Squares

1⅓ C. applesauce
2 env. unflavored gelatin
6 oz. pkg. fruit flavored gelatin

2 C. sugar
1 tsp. lemon juice
Sugar

Mix applesauce, unflavored and flavored gelatin, 2 C. sugar and lemon juice in a saucepan. Heat to boiling and boil 1 minute, stirring constantly. Fill a loaf pan half full with cold water. Pour out water and pour gelatin mixture into wet pan. Clean out saucepan with a rubber scraper. When loaf pan cools enough to touch, refrigerate for about 3 hours or until candy is firm. Cut candy into 1-inch squares (dip knife in cold water to keep from sticking). Lift each squares out and place on an ungreased cookie sheet. Let stand 8 hours to dry. After candy is dry, roll in sugar to coat all sides.

Peanut Brittle

2 C. sugar
¼ tsp. salt

1 C. white Karo
1 C. water

Cook above to 234° on candy thermometer. Add 3 C. raw peanuts. Cook 8 minutes, stirring all the time. Add 2 T. butter. Cook to 300°. Remove from fire; add 1 tsp. vanilla and stir. Add 2 tsp. soda, stir 15 seconds and pour onto buttered cookie sheet to cool. This will foam so use care when handling. After cool, break into pieces.

Peanut Brittle

1 C. white sugar
1 C. white corn syrup

2 C. raw peanuts

Boil all ingredients in deep pan. Boil to 280° on candy thermometer. Remove from heat. Add 1 T. soda. Stir. Will foam. Quickly pour onto buttered pan. Cool. Break into pieces.

Real Easy Fudge

1 stick oleo
12 oz. pkg. chocolate chips
2 eggs

1 lb. powdered sugar (3½ C.)
1 tsp. vanilla
Chopped nuts (opt.)

Do not change even one ingredient or procedure. Use about 10½ × 7-inch pan. Melt one stick oleo with 12 oz. pkg. chocolate morsels (over hot water). In a separate bowl beat 2 eggs until frothy. Beat them and 1 lb. box powdered sugar into the melted chocolate and oleo. Add 1 tsp. vanilla and nuts. Pour into a buttered pan and place in refrigerator until set. Cut and serve.

Cracker Candy

2 C. sugar
½ C. milk
¼ lb. soda crackers (finey crushed)

1 heaping tsp. peanut butter
1 tsp. vanilla

Combine sugar and milk; bring to a boil. Add crackers, peanut butter and vanilla. Stir well and let stand for 5 minutes. Beat and pour into a buttered 8 × 8 × 2 square inch pan. Cool in refrigerator. Cut into squares.

Fudge

1 lb. Velveeta cheese	1 tsp. vanilla
4 lbs. powdered sugar	1 C. cocoa
1 lb. butter (margarine)	Walnuts (if cheap)

Melt cheese and butter. Sift together cocoa and powdered sugar. Combine and add vanilla and nuts. Spread fudge mixture on a buttered cookie sheet. Let set.

Apple Crisp

¾ C. sugar	1⅓ C. brown sugar
½ tsp. cinnamon	½ C. butter
1 C. flour	

Slice skinned apples in a pie pan about half full. Spread sugar and cinnamon over them. Mix flour, brown sugar and butter together. Spread over apples. Bake at 375° for 30-40 minutes.

Penuche Candy

2 C. brown sugar
1 C. white sugar
½ C. milk
1 C. cream

Butter size of a walnut
1 C. nut meats (your choice)
1 tsp. vanilla
Pinch salt

Combine ingredients and boil, stirring constantly, to the soft ball stage. Take from heat and beat until cool and creamy. Add nuts and pour into a greased platter to cool.

Peanut Butter Fudge

1 C. white sugar
1 C. brown sugar
Pinch of salt
½ C. peanut butter

2 T. butter
1 T. vanilla
1 C. marshmallows
¼ C. evaporated milk

Cook sugar, butter and milk to a soft ball - 240°. Add salt, vanilla and mix. Add marshmallows and peanut butter. Remove from heat and beat until thick. Pour into pan and let stand until hard.

Brown Sugar Fudge

2 C. brown sugar
1 C. white sugar
1 C. light cream

½ C. butter
1 tsp. vanilla
1 C. chopped nuts

Combine sugars, cream and butter. Cook to softball stage (238°), stirring frequently; add vanilla. Cook to lukewarm (110°). Beat till mixture loses its gloss. Stir in nuts and pour into buttered 10×6×1½-inch pan. Cool and cut in squares.

Peanut Brittle

2 C. sugar
1 C. water
2 T. corn syrup
2 T. butter

1 tsp. baking soda
1/8 tsp. salt
1 C. peanuts

Combine sugar, corn syrup and water; cook to 290°. Just before taking off, add peanuts. Take off and add soda, salt and butter; stir in quickly. Pour out on well greased pan and spread thin. When cool, break up.

Popcorn Candy

3 qts. popcorn (or there-abouts)
1¼ C. sugar
1¼ C. molasses

½ tsp. salt
1½ T. melted butter

Use fresh crisp corn; spread out on buttered pan. Combine sugar, molasses, salt and melted butter in cooking pan. Cook to about 290° or hard crack stage. Pour over popcorn and spread thin, making sure all corn is covered. Break up when cold.

"Just For Notes"

MISCELLANEOUS

Miscellaneous

Bean Dip

10 C. water
4 C. pinto beans
2 C. onions (chopped fine)
1 C margarine
½ C. sharp Cheddar cheese
   (grated)

6 T. chili powder
6 T. bacon drippings
3 cloves garlic (chopped fine)
2 tsp. cumin
1/8 tsp. Tabasco

Combine water, beans, onions and bacon drippings. Cook slowly until beans are soft (3-3½ hours). Do not make too soupy. While still warm add in cheese. Tabasco and margarine; beat until smooth.

Tomato Jam

4½ lbs. ripe tomatoes (peeled)
4½ C. sugar
1 T. broken cinnamon

1½C. vinegar
½ tsp. allspice
1 tsp. cloves

Scald and peel tomatoes and then quarter them. Place in cooking pan and add sugar, vinegar and spices. Cook slowly till thickened and then put in jars.

May-Apples

Gather the May-apples from the stalks after, they have become a golden yellow. They are then buried in the ash hopper and left there a week or so or until the skins turn dark. The pulp on the inside is then ready to eat raw, just as it comes form the skins.

Tomato Catsup

1 gal. tomatoes
1 qt. vinegar (use less if too strong)
1 qt. sugar

½ tsp. red pepper
1 tsp. allspice
½ tsp. black pepper
1 T. salt

Crush tomatoes through colander or sieve. Combine all ingredients in a large pan and ccok slowly until thick enough. Bottle or put up in jars.

Popcorn Balls

Popcorn (more than gal.
   hot and crisp)
½ C. brown sugar
1½ C. white sugar

1½ C. water
½ tsp. salt
¾ C. corn syrup
1 tsp. vanilla

Combine in pan white sugar, brown sugar, water, salt, corn syrup and vanilla. Mix together and cook to 260° or hard ball stage. Pour over popcorn to open pan slowly. Butter hands and form into balls. This will make about 15-20 balls.

Egg Butter

Melt one quart of molasses in an iron skillet, then add six beaten egg yolks. Stir vigorously, then stir in nutmeg to suit the taste. Serve with hot bisuicts, or other hot breads.

Grandma's Elixers

POSSETT:
1 C. of milk, 1 T. of molasses. Let milk come to boiling point; add molasses, stir well, strain and serve.

PICK-ME-UP:
1 T. of powdered sugar, 1 egg, dash of salt, 1 T. of brandy. Separate the egg, beat yolk until thick and lemon colored; add the powdered sugar and brandy and heat again. THen blend the white of the eggs whipped to a stiff froth. This is so thick it may be eaten with a spoon.

Old Fashioned Bread & Butter pickles

Place 25 large cucumbers in cold water until crisp, then wipe dry and slice. Add 12 onions sliced and ½ C. of salt. Let stand for 1 hour. Do not drain. Add 1 quart vinegar and a little water, 2½ C. sugar, 2 T. mustard seed, 2 T. ginger root, 2 T. celery seed. boil all together for 5 minutes. While hot fill cans and seal.

Pigs Feet

PUt pigs feet in cold water. Scrape and clean well. Place in a pot and cover with salted water. Boil till the meat will slip from the bone. Can then be eaten in several different ways; baked with something else or just eaten as is.

Hot Chocolate Syrup

1 C. sugar
⅓ C. cocoa
1 T. butter

2 T. corn syrup
½ tsp. vanilla
1/8 tsp. salt

Melt butter in pan; add cocoa and stir over low heat until melted. Add boiling water gradually. Add sugar and syrup. Cook for 5 minutes, stirring often. Add vanilla and salt. Very good on ice cream.

Watermelon Pickle

Ten pounds of watermelon rind boiled in pure water until tender; drain the water off and make a syrup of 2 lbs. of white sugar, 1 qt. vinegar, ½ an ounce of cloves, 1 once of cinnamon. The syrup to be poured over the rind boiling hot three days in succession.

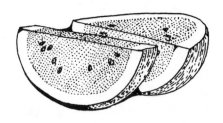

Head Cheese

Clean hogs head by removing snout, eyes, ears, brains and all skin. Trim off all fat. Cut heat in four pieces and soak in salt water (½ C. salt to 1 gal. water) for 3-5 hours to draw all blood. Drain from salt solution and wash well in clear water. Hearts, tongues and other meat trimmings may be cooked with the heat meat. Cover meat with hot water and boil until meat can be removed from the bones. Remove all the meat, strain broth and measure. One pint of broth is needed for 3 lbs. of chopped meat. To the broth and chopped meat add; 2 T. salt; 2 tsp. black pepper, 1 tsp. red pepper, 1 tsp. allspice and 2 tsp. cloves. Mix thoroughly and put in a loaf pan to set.

Nummy Chips

14 dill size cucumbers
8 C. sugar
1 qt. vinegar

1 tsp. salt (not iodized)
2 T. mixed pickling spices
 (tied in a bag)

Wash cucumbers well and pack in an enamel pan. Cover with boiling water. Pour this off each morning for 3 days and cover with fresh boiling water. On the fourth morning, slice the cucumbers into very thin slices and put back into the cleaned enamel pan. Combine sugar, vinegar, salt and mixed pickling spices. Boil hard. Pour hot syrup over sliced cucumbers. Each morning for three days pour off the sryup. Bring to boil and put back on the cucumbers. On the 4th day bring cucumbers and sryup to boil and put into hot sterilized jars. Wipe jar lips well and seal.

Ice Cream Toppings

HONEY NUT:
Mix together:
¾ C. honey   ⅓ C. chopped nuts or pecans

Makes about 1 C. of topping.

HONEY-BERRY:
Mix together:
¾ C. honey   ¾ C. strawberry jam or preserves

Makes 1½ C. of topping.

Butterscotch Sauce Ice Cream Topping

1 C. white corn syrup   1 C. water
1 C. white sugar   ½ tsp. vanilla
Pinch of salt (¼ tsp.)   ½ C. cream or 1 small can
1 C. brown sugar   evaporated milk

Mix corn syrup, white and brown sugar with 1 C. water. Simmer for 10 minutes. Cool to lukewarm. Stir in ½ C. cream or 1 small can evaporated milk and add salt and vanilla. Serve hot or cold over ice cream. If you have some left put in a jar and store in refrigerator.

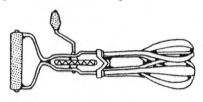

Salad Dressing

3 eggs (beaten)
⅔ C. sugar
2 T. oleo or butter
⅓ C. vinegar

¼ tsp. salt
1 tsp. mustard (opt.)
Dash of pepper, if desired)

Beat eggs, then add sugar, vinegar, salt and dash of pepper. Cook until thick (stir constantly). Add butter and beat well. Good for potato salad if thinned with some cream or Half & Half or better yet, mix this with about an equal amount of Miracle Whip or more. If making a small batch of salad you probably won't need all of it. Again, when mixing taste frequently and season accordingly. You can always add more sugar, vinegar, salt, pepper, etc.

Zucchini Jam

5½ C. grated zucchini
6 C. sugar
1 C. water

2 T. lemon juice
1 (20 oz.) can crushed pineapple
2 (3 oz. ea.) pkgs. Jello
(any flavor)

Boil 6 minutes zucchini, sugar and water. Add lemon juice and pineapple. Boil 6 minutes more. Add two 3 oz. each pkgs. Jello. Boil 6 minutes more. Pour hot mixture into jars; put on lid and screw band. Jars will seal without processing if you put on lids immediately after you pour in hot mixture.

Hot Fudge Sauce

1 C. sugar	1 C. water
2 T. (heaping) cornstarch	1 T. butter
¼ C. cocoa	½ tsp. vanilla

Mix first 3 ingredients well with spoon. Add water and butter and cook mixture until thick. Watch carefully and stir occasionally at beginning and continually near end. When thick, remove from heat and stir in vanilla. Serve over ice cream. Delicious!

Refrigerator Pickles

4 C. sugar	4 C. vinegar
½ C. salt	1½ tsp. turmeric
1½ tsp. celery seed	1½ tsp. mustard seed
Cucumbers (thinly sliced)	3 lg. onions (thinly sliced)

Mix all ingredients except cucumbers and onions. Do not heat. Place cucumbers and onions in a covered container. Pour brine over them. Refrigerate. Wait at least 5 days before using.

Tartar Sauce

1 pt. mayonnaise	½ green pepper
½ bunch parsley	1/16 bottole horseradish
¾ lb. onion	¼ bunch celery
½ pt. dill pickles	¼ oz. celery salt
¼ head cabbage	

Chop all of the above ingredients and blend thoroughly in blender. Makes 1 quart.

French Dressing

1½ C. salad oil
1½ C. sugar
½ bottle catsup (small size)

¼ C. vinegar
Salt and pepper

Beat together for 10 minutes and refrigerate.

Salad Dressing

½ C. sugar
½ C. vinegar
1 T. butter

1 beaten egg
1 C. sour cream

Bring sugar, vinegar and butter to a boil, then add egg and sour cream and boil until thick and smooth.

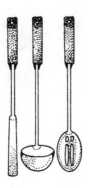

Caserole Sauce Mix

2 C. nonfat dry milk powder
¾ C. cornstarch
¼ C. powdered chicken bouillon
4 tsp. onion powder

1 tsp. dried thyme leaves
1 tsp. dried basil leaves
½ tsp. pepper

Use with chicken, tuna, macaroni and cheese. ¾ C. to a casserole.

Dill Pickles

1 C. sugar
1 C. vinegar
2 T. salt

Onion
Dill

Boil first 3 ingredients. Cut onion. Put slice in bottom of jar. Also head of dill. Fill jar with sliced cucumbers. Cover with above mixture and seal. Make sure syrup is real hot.

Need A Gift?

For

- Shower • Birthday • Mother's Day •
    - Anniversary • Christmas •

Turn Page for Order Form
(Order Now While Supply Lasts!)

To Order Copies Of

Flat-Out Dirt-Cheap Cookin'

Please send me _____ copies of **Flat-Out Dirt-Cheap Cookin'** at
$11.95 each. (Make checks payable to **QUIXOTE PRESS**.)

Name _____

Street _____

City _____State _____Zip _____

Send Orders To:
Quixote Press
R.R. #4, Box 33B • Blvd. Station
Sioux City, Iowa 51109

- -

To Order Copies Of

Flat-Out Dirt-Cheap Cookin'

Please send me _____ copies of **Flat-Out Dirt-Cheap Cookin'** at
$11.95 each. (Make checks payable to **QUIXOTE PRESS**.)

Name _____

Street _____

City _____State _____Zip _____

Send Orders To:
Quixote Press
R.R. #4, Box 33B • Blvd. Station
Sioux City, Iowa 51109

STANDARD ABBREVIATIONS

tsp. - teaspoon
T. - tablespoon
C. - cup
f.g. - few grains
pt. - pint
qt. - quart

d.b. - double boiler
B.P. - baking powder
oz. - ounce
lb. - pounds
pk. - peck
bu. - bushel

GUIDE TO WEIGHTS AND MEASURES

1 teaspoon - 60 drops
3 teaspoons - 1 tablespoon
2 tablespoons - 1 fluid ounce
4 tablespoons - ¼ cup
5⅓ tablespoons - ⅓ cup
8 tablespoons - ½ cup
16 tablespoons - 1 cup

1 pound - 16 ounces
1 cup - ½ pint
2 cups - 1 pint
4 cups - 1 quart
4 quarts - 1 gallon
8 quarts - 1 peck
4 pecks - 1 bushel

SUBSTITUTIONS AND EQUIVALENTS

2 tablespoons of fat - 1 ounce
1 cup of fat - ½ pound
1 pound of butter -2 cups
1 cup of hydrogenated fat plus ½ t. salt - 1 cup butter
2 cups sugar - 1 pound
2½ cups packed brown sugar - 1 pound
1⅓ cups packed brown sugar - 1 cup of granulated sugar
3½ cups of powdered sugar - 1 pound
4 cups sifted all-purpose flour - 1 pound
4½ cups sifted cake flour - 1 pound
1 ounce bitter chocolate - 1 square
4 tablespoons cocoa plus 2 teaspoon butter - 1 ounce of bitter chocolate
1 cup egg whites - 8 to 10 whites
1 cup egg yolks - 12 to 14 yolks
16 marshmallows - ¼ pound
1 tablespoon cornstarch - 2 tablespoons flour for thickening
1 tablespoon vinegar or lemon juice + 1 cup milk - 1 cup sour milk
10 graham crackers - 1 cup fine crumbs
1 cup whipping cream - 2 cups whipped
1 cup evaporated milk - 3 cups whipped
1 lemon - 3 to 4 tablespoons juice
1 orange - 6 to 8 tablespoons juice
1 cup uncooked rice - 3 to 4 cups cooked rice

SUBSTITUTIONS

FOR	YOU CAN USE. . .
1 T. cornstarch	2 T. flour OR 1½ T. quick cooking tapioca
1 C. cake flour	1 C. less 2 T. all-purpose flour
1 C. all-purpose flour	1 C. plus 2 T. cake flour
1 sq. chocolate	3 T. cocoa & 1 T. fat
1 C. melted shortening	1 C. salad oil (may not be substituted for solid shortening)
1 C. milk	½ C. evaporated milk & ½ C. water
1 C. sour milk or buttermilk	1 T. lemon juice or vinegar & enough sweet milk to measure 1 C.
1 C. heavy cream	⅔ C. milk & ⅓ C. butter
Sweetened condensed milk	No substitution
1 egg	2 T. dried whole egg & 2 T. water
1 tsp. baking powder	¼ tsp. baking soda & 1 tsp. cream of tartar OR ¼ tsp. baking soda & ½ C. sour milk, buttermilk or molasses; reduce other liquid ½ C.
1 C. sugar	1 C. honey; reduce other liquid ¼ C.; reduce baking temperature by 25°
1 C. miniature marshmallows	About 10 large marshmallows (cut-up)
1 medium onion (2½-inch diameter) . . .	2 T. instant minced onion OR 1 tsp. onion powder OR 2 T. onion salt; reduce salt 1 tsp.
1 garlic clove	1/8 tsp. garlic powder OR ¼ tsp. garlic salt; reduce salt 1/8 tsp.
1 T. fresh herbs	1 tsp. dried herbs OR ¼ tsp. powdered herbs OR ½ tsp. herb salt; reduce salt ¼ tsp.

Protein Content and Caloric Value of Foods for Your Diet

Food	Oz.	Approximate Measure	Protein	Calories
Lamb				
Chops				
Loin or				
rib	4	1 loin or 2 rib 1-inch thick	17.9	421
Shoulder	4	Piece 4x3x5/8-inch	18.7	348
Roasts				
Leg	4	Slice 4x3x½-inch	21.6	276
Shoulder	4	Slice 5x3x½-inch	18.7	348
Pork, fresh				
Chops and steaks				
Leg (ham)	4	Piece 3½x3x½-inch	18.2	408
Loin	4	Chop ¾-inch thick	19.7	349
Shoulder	4	Piece 4½x3½x3/8-inch	16.1	464
Roasts				
Boston butt	4	Slice 4½x3½x3/8-inch	19.9	327
Loin	4	Slice ¾-inch thick	19.7	349
Tenderloin	4	2 pieces 1-inch dia.x3-inches long	23.9	172
Pork, cured				
Bacon,				
Canadian				
style	1	Slice 2¼-inch diameter by 3/16-inch thick	6.6	68
Ham				
(boiled)	2	Slice 4¼x4x1/8-inch	10.6	147
Veal				
Chops				
Loin	4	Chop 5/8-inch thick	23.0	211
Rib	4	Chop ¾-inch thick	22.6	241
Roasts				
Leg	4	Slice 4x2½x½-inch	22.9	223
Loin	4	Slice 4x2½x½-inch	23.0	211
Rib	4	Slice 4x2½x½-inch	22.6	241
Shoulder	4	Slice 5x3x½-inch	23.3	202
Steaks				
Cutlet				
(round)	4	Piece 4x2½x½-inch	23.4	191
Shoulder	4	Piece 5x3x½-inch	23.3	202
Sirloin	4	Piece 4x2½x½-inch	23.0	211
Stew				
(breast)	4	4 pieces 2½x1x1-inch	22.0	271
Variety Meats				
Brains (beef)	4	2 pieces 2½x1½x1-inch	12.6	152
Heart (avg.)	4	⅓ ht. 3-inch dia. x 3½-inch long	19.7	157
Kidney (avg.)	4	3 slices 3¼x2½x¼-inch	20.0	161
Liver				
Beef	3	2 slices 3x2½x3/8-inch	17.7	119
Lamb	3	2 slices 3½x2x3/8-inch	18.9	118
Pork	3	2 slices 3½x2x3/8-inch	17.7	116
Veal	3	2 slices 3x2½x3/8-inch	17.1	122
Sweetbread	4	Piece 4x3x¾-inch	18.2	216
Tongue	3	3 slices 3x2x¼-inch	15.7	191

Protein Content and Caloric Value of Foods for Your Diet

Food	Oz.	Approximate Measure	Protein	Calories
Sausages and Cooked Specialties				
Bologna	1	Slice 4½ dia. x ½-inch thick	4.4	65
Frankfurter	2	2 5½-inch long x ¾-inch dia.	9.1	121
Liver sausage	1	Slice 3-inch dia. x ¼-inch thick	5.0	77
Luncheon meat	1	Slice 4x3½x1/8-inch	4.6	81
Vienna sausage	1	2 pieces 2-inch long x ¾-inch diameter	5.8	76
Poultry				
Chicken				
Liver	3	4 avg.	19.9	122
Roast				
Breast	3	½ breast	21.0	110
Leg	2½	1 avg.	14.7	88
Thigh	2½	1 avg.	15.8	95
Wing	1	1 avg.	7.0	37
Stewed				
Dark meat	3½	½ cup (diced)	23.1	139
Light meat	3	½ cup (diced)	20.3	106
Turkey				
Roast				
Dark meat	3½	Slice 4x3x½-inch	23.2	177
Light meat	3½	Slice 4x3x½-inch	24.5	139
Fish				
Bass	4	1 small fish	27.3	113
Clams	3½	5 medium	12.8	77
Cod	3½	Piece 4x2¼x¾-inch	16.5	70
Crab (canned)	3	⅔ cup	16.1	94
Finnan haddie	3½	¾ cup	23.2	96
Flounder	3½	Piece 4x3x3/8-inch	19.0	79
Haddock	3½	Piece 3½x3x¾-inch	17.2	72
Halibut	4	Piece 4x3x½-inch	20.4	133
Herring, fresh	4	1 fish 7-inches long	22.8	163
Lobster				
Canned	3	½ cup	15.6	74
Fresh	2½	1 avg.	12.2	63
Mackerel	2½	¼ fish 7-inches long	14.3	119
Oysters	3½	5 medium	6.0	50
Perch	4	2 fish 4½-inches long	23.4	102
Salmon				
Canned	3½	⅔ cup	24.7	203
Fresh	3	Piece 2½x2½x7/8-inch	15.7	196
Shrimp (canned)	2	3/8 cup or 12 pieces 1-inch dia.	10.7	49
Trout	3	Piece 6-inches long	16.1	80
White fish	4	Piece 3¼-inchx3x½-inch	25.2	165
Milk and Dairy Products				
Butter	⅓		.1	73
Cheese, cottage	2	¼ cup	9.6	51
Cream, coffee	½	1 T.	.4	29

Protein Content and Caloric Value of Foods for Your Diet

Food	Approx. Weight (Oz.)	Approximate Measure (Gm.)	Protein	Calories
Milk				
Buttermilk	7	1 glass	7.0	72
Evaporated	4	½ cup	8.4	167
Skim	7	1 glass	7.0	72
Whole	7	1 glass	7.0	138
Eggs	1⅔	1 medium	6.4	79
Potatoes				
White	2	1 small 2½-inch long x 2-inch dia.	1.2	51
Vegetables				
Artichokes	3½	½ large	2.9	63
Asparagus	3½	7 stalks 6-inches long	2.3	27
Beans, string	3½	⅔ cup	2.4	42
Beet greens	3½	½ cup	2.0	33
Beets	3½	⅔ cup or 2 1¾-inch dia.	1.6	46
Broccoli	3½	2 stalks 5-inches long	3.3	37
Brussels sprts.	3½	⅔ cup	4.4	58
Cabbage	3½	1/5 head 4½-inch dia.	1.4	29
Carrots	3½	2 carrots 5-inch long	1.2	45
Cauliflower	3½	⅔ cup	2.4	31
Celery	½	Piece 8½-inch long or 2 hts.	.2	3
Chard, Swiss	3½	½ cup	1.4	25
Chicory	1	10 small leaves	.4	7
Cucumbers	2	8 slices 1/8-inch thick	.4	7
Eggplant	2	Slices 3½-inch dia x 3/8-inch thick	.7	17
Endive, French	2	2 stalks	.8	11
Green pepper	½	½ cup or piece 4x1¾-inch	.2	4
Kohlrabi	3½	⅔ cup (diced)	2.1	36
Lettuce				
Head	3½	¼ head 4-inch diameter	1.2	18
	½	1 leaf	.2	3
Leaf	½	2 leaves	.1	2
Mushrooms	3½	5 caps 2¼-inch dia.	2.6	15
Okra	2	5 pods	1.0	21
Onions				
Dried	3	1 onion 2-inch dia.	1.2	42
Green	½	3 medium	.2	7
Parsley		2 sprigs	.1	1
Pumpkin	3½	½ cup	1.2	36
Radishes	1	3 radishes 1-inch dia.	.4	7
Rutabagas	3½	½ cup	1.1	41
Sauerkraut	3½	⅔ cup	1.1	18
Spinach	3½	¾ cup	2.3	25
Squash				
Summer	3½	½ cup	.6	19
Winter	3½	½ cup	1. 5	44
Tomatoes				
Canned	3½	½ cup	1.2	25
Fresh	3½	1 tomato 2-inch dia.	1.0	23
Juice, canned	4	½ cup	1.2	28
Turnip greens	3½	½ cup	2.9	37

Protein Content and Caloric Value of Foods for Your Diet

Food	Oz.	Approximate Measure	Protein	Calories
Turnips				
White	3½	⅔ cup	1.1	35
Yellow (see	rutabagas)			
Pickles				
Olives				
Green	1/6	1 medium	.1	7
Ripe	½	1 large	.2	23
Pickles				
Dill	2	½ pickle 5-inches long x1½-inch diameter	.3	7
Sweet	½	1 pickle 2½-inches long x¾-inch diameter	.2	21
BREAD AND CEREAL PRODUCTS				
Cereals				
Bran, whole	⅔	⅓ cup	2.5	67
Cornflakes	½	⅔ cup	1.3	56
Farina,				
enriched	⅔	½ cup (sc. 2 T. dry)	2.3	71
Oatmeal	⅔	½ cup (¼ cup dry)	3.1	77
Rice				
Puffed	⅓	¾ cup	.7	36
White	1	⅔ cup (2 T. dry)	2.3	105
Wheat				
Flakes	⅔	¾ cup	2.4	74
Puffed	⅓	¾ cup	1.2	37
Shredded	1	1 biscuit	2.9	103
Breads				
Rye	⅔	Slice 4x3½x½-inch	1.2	50
Wheat				
Melba toast	1/6	Slice 3x2x¼-inch	.6	19
White, enrch	⅔	1 slice (commercial) thin	1.6	50
Whole wheat	⅔	1 slice (commercial) thin	1.8	50
Crackers				
Graham	½	1 cracker 3-inch square	1.0	54
Saltine	½	1 cracker 2-inch square	.4	17
Soda	1/5	1 cracker 2¾x2½-inch	.6	25
Zwieback	¼	1 piece 3¼x1¼x½-inch	.9	33
Beverages				
Carbonated	6	1 small bottle		82
Coffee, black			0	0
Tea, plain			0	0
Fruits				
Apples	3½	1 apple 2¼-inch diameter	.3	65
Apricots	1	1 medium	.4	20
Blackberries	3½	¾ cup	1.2	62
Blueberries	3½	⅔ cup	.6	68
Cantaloupe	4	¼ melon 5-inch diameter	.8	29
Cherries,				
sweet	3½	15 cherries 7/8-inch diameter	1.2	87
Grapefruit	3½	½ medium 3 5/8-inch dia.	.5	44
Grapes				
Concord	3½	34 avg.	1.4	78
Green				
seedless	3½	40 small	.8	74
Malaga or				
Tokay	3½	21 avg.	.8	74

Protein Content and Caloric Value of Foods for Your Diet

Honeydew melon	4	1½-inch slice, 7-inch melon	.9	48
Oranges	3½	½ orange 4-inch diameter	.9	52
Peaches	3½	1 medium	.5	51
Pears	3½	1 small	.7	70
Pineapple	3½	1 slice 4-inch diameter x ½-inch thick	.4	58
Plums	2½	1 plum 1¾-inch dia.	.5	39
Raspberries	3	⅔ cup	1.1	64
Strawberries	3½	10 strawberries 1-inch dia.	.8	41
Watermelon	5	½ slice 6-inch dia. x ¾-inch thick	.8	51
FRUIT JUICES				
Grapefruit, canned	4	½ cup	.6	49
Orange	4	½ cup	.7	66
Pineapple canned	4	½ cup	.4	65
Tomato (see	vegetables)			

HOW MANY DROPS IN A "DASH"?
Here, a cook's guide to the most-often-called-for food measures and equivalents

How many cups of berries in a pint? How many slices of bread make a half cup of crumbs? For two tablespoons of orange peel, will you need more than one orange? You'll find the answers to these questions and lots more in this handy kitchen chart.

EQUIVALENT MEASURES

Dash	2 to 3 drops or less than 1/8 teaspoon
1 tablespoon	3 teaspoons
¼ cup	4 tablespoons
⅓ cup	5 tablespoons plus 1 teaspoon
½ cup	8 tablespoons
1 cup	16 tablespoons
1 pint	2 cups
1 quart	4 cups
1 gallon	4 quarts
1 peck	8 quarts
1 bushel	4 pecks
1 pound	16 ounces

FOOD EQUIVALENTS

Apples *1 pound*	3 medium (3 cups sliced)
Bananas *1 pound*	3 medium (1⅓ cups mashed)
Berries *1 pint*	1¾ cups
Bread *1 pound loaf*	14 to 20 slices
Bread crumbs, fresh *1 slice bread with crust*	½ cup bread crumbs
Broth, chicken or beef *1 cup*	1 bouillon cube or 1 envelope bouillon or 1 teaspoon instant bouillon dissolved in 1 cup boiling water
Butter or margarine *¼ pound stick*	½ cup
Cheese *¼ pound*	1 cup, shredded
Cheese, cottage *8 ounces*	1 cup
Cheese, cream *3 ounces*	6 tablespoons
Chocolate, unsweetened *1 ounce*	1 square
Chocolate, semi-sweet pieces *6 ounce package*	1 cup

QUANTITIES TO SERVE 100 PEOPLE

Coffee	—3 lbs.
Loaf Sugar	—3 lbs.
Cream	—3 qts.
Whipping Cream	—4 pts.
Milk	—6 gallons
Fruit	—2½ gallons
Fruit Juice	—4 (No. 10 ea.) cans (26 lbs.)
Tomato Juice	—4 (No. 10 ea.) cans (26 lbs.)
Soup	—5 gallons
Oysters	—18 qts.
Weiners	—25 lbs.
Meatloaf	—24 lbs.
Ham	—40 lbs.
Beef	—40 lbs.
Roast Pork	—40 lbs.
Hamburger	—30-36 lbs.
Chicken For Chicken Pie	—40 lbs.
Potatoes	—35 lbs.
Scalloped Potatoes	—5 gallon
Vegetables	—4 (No. 10 ea.) cans (26 lbs.)
Baked Beans	—5 gallon
Beets	—30 lbs.
Cauliflower	—18 lbs.
Cabbage For Slaw	—20 lbs.
Carrots	—33 lbs.
Bread	—10 loaves
Rolls	—200
Butter	—3 lbs.
Potato Salad	—12 qts.
Fruit Salad	—20 qts.
Vegetable Salad	—20 qts.
Lettuce	—20 heads
Salad Dressing	—3 qts.
Pies	—18
Cakes	—8
Ice Cream	—4 gallons
Cheese	—3 lbs.
Olives	—1¾ lbs.
Pickles	—2 qts.
Nuts	—3 lbs. sorted

To Serve 50 People, Divide by 2
To Serve 25 People, Divide by 4

THE KITCHEN
General Household Hints

SALT

If stew is too salty, add raw cut potatoes and discard once they have cooked and absorbed the salt. Another remedy is to add a teaspoon each of cider vinegar and sugar. Or, simply add sugar.

If soup or stew is too sweet, add salt. For a main dish or vegetable, add a teaspoon of cider vinegar.

GRAVY

For pale gravy, color with a few drops of Kitchen Bouquet. Or to avoid the problem in the first place, brown the flour well before adding the liquid. This also helps prevent lumpy gravy.

To make gravy smooth, keep a jar with a mixture of equal parts of flour and cornstarch. Put 3-4 T. of this mixture in another jar and add some water. Shake, and in a few minutes you will have a smooth paste for gravy.

To remedy greasy gravy, add a small amount of baking soda.

For quick thickener for gravies, add some instant potatoes to your gravy and it will thicken beautifully.

VEGETABLES

If fresh vegetables are wilted or blemished, pick off the brown edges. Sprinkle with cool water, wrap in towel and refrigerate for an hour or so.

Perk up soggy lettuce by adding lemon juice to a bowl of cold water and soak for an hour in the refrigerator.

Lettuce and celery will crisp up fast if you place it in a pan of cold water and add a few sliced potatoes.

If vegetables are overdone, put the pot in a pan of cold water. Let it stand from 15 minutes to ½ hour without scraping pan.

By lining the crisper section of your refrigerator with newspaper and wrapping vegetables with it, moisture will be absorbed and your vegetables will stay fresher longer.

EGGS

If you shake the egg and you hear a rattle, you can be sure it's stale. A really fresh egg will float and a stale one will sink.

If you are making deviled eggs and want to slice it perfectly, dip the knife in water first. The slice will be smooth with no yolk sticking to the knife.

The white of an egg is easiest to beat when it's at room temperature. So leave it out of the refrigerator about ½ hour before using it.

To make light and fluffy scrambled eggs, add a little water while beating the eggs.

Add vinegar to the water while boiling eggs. Vinegar helps to seal the egg, since it acts on the calcium in the shell.

To make quick-diced eggs, take your potato masher and go to work on a boiled egg.

If you wrap each egg in aluminum foil before boiling it, the shell won't crack when it's boiling.

To make those eggs go further when making scrambled eggs for a crowd, add a pinch of baking powder and 2 tsp. of water per egg.

A great trick for peeling eggs the easy way - when they are finished boiling, turn off the heat and just let them sit in the pan with the lid on for about 5 minutes. Steam will build up under the shell and they will just fall away.

Or, quickly rinse hot hard-boiled eggs in cold water, and the shells will be easier to remove.

When you have saved a lot of egg yolks from previous recipes; use them in place of whole eggs for baking or thickening. Just add 2 yolks for every whole egg.

Fresh or hard-boiled? Spin the egg. If it wobbles, it is raw - if it spins easily, it's hard-boiled.

Add a few drops of vinegar to the water when poaching an egg to keep it from running all over the pan.

Add 1 T. of water per egg white to increase the quantity of beaten egg white when making meringue.

Try adding eggshells to coffee after it has perked, for a better flavor.

POTATOES

Overcooked potatoes can become soggy when the milk is added. Sprinkle with dry powdered milk for the fluffiest mashed potatoes ever.

To hurry up baked potatoes, boil in salted water for 10 minutes, then place in a very hot oven. Or, cut potatoes in half and place them face down on a baking sheet in the oven to make the baking time shorter.

When making potato pancakes, add a little sour cream to keep potatoes from discoloring.

Save some of the water in which the potatoes were boiled - add to some powdered milk and use when mashing. This restores some of the nutrients that were lost in the cooking process.

Use a couple of tablespoons of cream cheese in place of butter for your potatoes; try using sour cream instead of milk when mashing.

ONIONS

To avoid tears when peeling onions, peel them under cold water or refrigerate before chopping.

For sandwiches to go in lunchboxes, sprinkle with dried onion. They will have turned into crisp pieces by lunchtime.

Peel and quarter onions. Place one layer deep in a pan and freeze. Quickly pack in bags or containers while frozen. Use as needed, chopping onions while frozen, with a sharp knife.

TOMATOES

Keep tomatoes in storage with stems pointed downward and they will retain their freshness longer.

Sunlight doesn't ripen tomatoes. It's the warmth that makes them ripen. So find a warm spot near the stove or dishwasher where they can get a little heat.

Save the juice from canned tomatoes in ice cube trays. When frozen, store in plastic bags in freezer for cooking use or for tomato drinks.

To improve the flavor of inexpensive tomato juice, pour a 46-ounce can of it into a refrigerator jar and add one chopped green onion and a cut-up stalk of celery.

ROCK-HARD BROWN SUGAR

Add a slice of soft bread to the package of brown sugar, close the bag tightly, and in a few hours the sugar will be soft again. If you need it in a hurry, simply grate the amount called for with a hand grater. Or, put brown sugar and a cup of water (do not add to the sugar, set it alongside of it) in a covered pan. Place in the oven (low heat) for awhile. Or, buy liquid brown sugar.

THAWING FROZEN MEAT

Seal the meat in a plastic bag and place in a bowl of very warm water. Or, put in a bag and let cold water run over it for an hour or so.

CAKED OR CLOGGED SALT

Tightly wrap a piece of aluminum foil around the salt shaker. This will keep the dampness out of the salt. To prevent clogging, keep 5 to 10 grains of rice inside your shaker.

SOGGY POTATO CHIPS, CEREAL AND CRACKERS

If potato chips lose their freshness, place under broiler for a few moments. Care must be taken not to brown them. You can crisp soggy cereal and crackers by putting them on a cookie sheet and heating for a few minutes in the oven.

PANCAKE SYRUP

To make an inexpensive syrup for pancakes, save small amounts of leftover jams and jellies in a jar. Or, fruit-flavored syrup can be made by adding 2 C. sugar to 1 C. of any kind of fruit juice and cooking until it boils.

EASY TOPPING

A good topping for gingerbread, coffeecake, etc., can easily be made by freezing the syrup from canned fruit and adding 1 T. of butter and 1 T. of lemon juice to 2 C. of syrup. Heat until bubbly, and thicken with 2 T. of flour.

TASTY CHEESE SANDWICHES

Toast cheese sandwiches in a frying pan lightly greased with bacon fat for a delightful new flavor.

HURRY-UP HAMBURGERS

Poke a hole in the middle of the patties while shaping them. The burgers will cook faster and the holes will disappear when done.

SHRINKLESS LINKS

Boil sausage links for about 8 minutes before frying and they will shrink less and not break at all. Or, you can roll them lightly in flour before frying.

FROZEN BREAD

Put frozen bread loaves in a clean brown paper bag and place for 5 minutes in a 325° oven to thaw completely.

REMOVING THE CORN SILK

Dampen a paper towel or terry cloth and brush downward on the cob of corn. Every strand should come off.

NUTS

To quickly crack open a large amount of nuts, put in a bag and gently hammer until they are cracked open. Then remove nutmeats with a pick.

If nuts are stale, place them in the oven at 250° and leave them there for 5 to 10 minutes. The heat will revive them.

PREVENTING BOIL-OVERS

Add a lump of butter or a few teaspoons of cooking oil to the water. Rice, noodles or spaghetti will not boil over or stick together.

SOFTENING BUTTER

Soften butter quickly by grating it. Or heat a small pan and place it upside-down over the butter dish for several minutes. Or place in the microwave for a few seconds.

MEASURING STICKY LIQUIDS

Before measuring honey or syrup, oil the cup with cooking oil and rinse in hot water.

SCALDED MILK

Add a bit of sugar (without stirring) to milk to prevent it from scorching.

Rinse the pan in cold water before scalding milk, and it will be much easier to clean.

TENDERIZING MEAT

Boiled meat: Add a tablespoon of vinegar to the cooking water.

Tough meat or game: Make a marinade of equal parts cooking vinegar and heated bouillon. Marinate for 2 hours.

Steak: Simply rub in a mixture of cooking vinegar and oil. Allow to stand for 2 hours.

Chicken: To stew an old hen, soak it in vinegar for several hours before cooking. It will taste like a spring chicken.

INSTANT WHITE SAUCE

Blend together 1 C. soft butter and 1 C. flour. Spread in an ice cube tray, chill well, cut into 16 cubes before storing in a plastic bag in the freezer. For medium-thick sauce, drop 1 cube into 1 C. of milk and heat slowly, stirring as it thickens.

UNPLEASANT COOKING ODORS

While cooking vegetables that give off unpleasant odors, simmer a small pan of vinegar on top of the stove. Or, add vinegar to the cooking water. To remove the odor of fish from cooking and serving implements, rinse in vinegar water.

DON'T LOSE THOSE VITAMINS

Put vegetables in water after the water boils - not before - to be sure to preserve all the vegetables' vitamins.

CLEAN AND DEODORIZE YOUR CUTTING BOARD

Bleach it clean with lemon juice. Take away strong odors like onion with baking soda. Just rub in.

KEEP THE COLOR IN BEETS

If you find that your beets tend to lose color when you boil them, add a little lemon juice.

NO-SMELL CABBAGE

Two things to do to keep cabbage smell from filling the kitchen; don't overcook it (keep it crisp) and put half a lemon in the water when you boil it.

A GREAT ENERGY SAVER

When you're near the end of the baking time, turn the oven off and keep the door closed. The heat will stay the same long enough to finish baking your cake or pie and you'll save all that energy.

GRATING CHEESE

Chill the cheese before grating and it will take much less time.

SPECIAL LOOKING PIES

Give a unique look to your pies by using pinking shears to cut the dough. Make a pinked lattice crust!

REMOVING HAM RIND

Before placing ham in the roasting pan, slit rind lengthwise on the underside. The rind will peel away as the ham cooks, and can be easily removed.

SLUGGISH CATSUP

Push a drinking straw to the bottom of the bottle and remove. This admits enough air to start the catsup flowing.

UNMOLDING GELATIN

Rinse the mold pan in cold water and coat with salad oil. The oil will give the gelatin a nice luster and it will easily fall out of the mold.

LEFTOVER SQUASH

Squash that is leftover can be improved by adding some maple syrup before reheated.

NO-SPILL CUPCAKES

An ice cream scoop can be used to fill cupcake papers without spilling.

SLICING CAKE OR TORTE

Use dental floss to slice evenly and cleanly through a cake or torte - simply stretch a length of the floss taut and press down through the cake.

CANNING PEACHES
Don't bother to remove skins when canning or freezing peaches. They will taste better and be more nutritious with the skin on.

ANGEL FOOD COOKIES
Stale angel food cake can be cut into ½-inch slices and shaped with cookie cutters to make delicious "cookies". Just toast in the oven for a few minutes.

HOW TO CHOP GARLIC
Chop in a small amount of salt to prevent pieces from sticking to the knife or chopping board then pulverize with the tip or the knife.

EXCESS FAT ON SOUPS OR STEWS
Remove fat from stews or soups by refrigerating and eliminating fat as it rises and hardens on the surface. Or add lettuce leaves to the pot - the fat will cling to them. Discard lettuce before serving.

BROILED MEAT DRIPPINGS
Place a piece of bread under the rack on which you are broiling meat. Not only will this absorb the dripping fat, but it will reduce the chance of the fat catching on fire.

FAKE SOUR CREAM
To cut down on calories, run cottage cheese through the blender. It can be flavored with chives, extracts, etc., and used in place of mayonnaise.

BROWNED BUTTER
Browning brings out the flavor of the butter, so only half as much is needed for seasoning vegetables if it is browned before it is added.

COOKING DRIED BEANS
When cooking dried beans, add salt after cooking; if salt is added at the start it will slow the cooking process.

TASTY CARROTS
Adding sugar and horseradish to cooked carrots improves their flavor.

CARROT MARINADE
Marinate carrot sticks in dill pickle juice.

CLEAN CUKES
A ball of nylon net cleans and smooths cucumbers when making pickles.

FRESH GARLIC
Peel garlic and store in a covered jar of vegetable oil. The garlic will stay fresh and the oil will be nicely flavored for salad dressings.

LEFTOVER WAFFLES
Freeze waffles that are left; they can be reheated in the toaster.

FLUFFY RICE
Rice will be fluffier and whiter if you add 1 tsp. of lemon juice to each quart of water.

NUTRITIOUS RICE
Cook rice in liquid saved from cooking vegetables to add flavor and nutrition. A nutty taste can be achieved by adding wheat germ to the rice.

PERFECT NOODLES
When cooking noodles, bring required amount of water to a boil, add noodles, turn heat off and allow to stand for 20 minutes. This prevents overboiling and the chore of stirring. Noodles won't stick to the pan with this method.

EASY CROUTONS
Make delicious croutons for soup or salad by saving toast, cutting into cubes, and sauteeing in garlic butter.

BAKED FISH
To keep fish from sticking to the pan, bake on a bed of chopped onion, celery and parsley. This also adds a nice flavor to the fish.

NON-STICKING BACON

Roll a package of bacon into a tube before opening. This will loosen the slices and keep them from sticking together.

TASTY HOT DOGS

Boil hot dogs in sweet pickle juice and a little water for a different tate.

GOLDEN-BROWN CHICKEN

For golden-brown fried chicken, roll it in powdered milk instead of flour.

DOUBLE BOILER HINT

Toss a few marbles in the bottom of a double boiler. When the water boils down, the noise will let you know!

FLOUR PUFF

Keep a powder puff in your flour container to easily dust your rolling pin or pastry board.

JAR LABELS

Attach canning labels to the lids instead of the sides of jelly jars, to prevent the chore of removing the labels when the contents are gone.

DIFFERENT MEATBALLS

Try using crushed corn flakes or corn bread instead of bread crumbs in a meatball recipe or use onion-flavored potato chips.

CLEAN-UP TIPS

APPLIANCES

To rid yellowing from white appliances try this. Mix together ½ C. bleach, ¼ C. baking soda, and 4 C. warm water. Apply with a sponge and let set for 10 minutes. Rinse and dry thoroughly.

Instead of using commercial waxes, shine with rubbing alcohol.

For quick clean-ups, rub with equal parts water and household ammonia.

Or, try club soda. It cleans and polishes at the same time.

BLENDER
Fill part way with hot water and add a drop of detergent. Cover and turn it on for a few seconds. Rinse and drain dry.

BREADBOARDS
To rid cutting board of onion, garlic or fish smell, cut a lime or lemon in two and rub the surface with the cut side of the fruit.

Or, make a paste of baking soda and water and apply generously. Rinse.

COPPER POTS
Fill a spray bottle with vinegar and add 3 T. of salt. Spray solution liberally on copper pot. Let set for awhile, then simply rub clean.

Dip lemon halves in salt and rub.

Or, rub with Worcestershire sauce or catsup. The tarnish will disappear.

Clean with toothpaste and rinse.

BURNT AND SCORCHED PANS
Sprinkle burnt pans liberally with baking soda, adding just enough water to moisten. Let stand for several hours. You can generally lift the burned portions right out of the pan.

Stubborn stains on non-stick cookware can be removed by boiling 2 T. of baking soda, ½ C. vinegar, and 1 C. water for 10 minutes. Re-season with salad oil.

CAST-IRON SKILLETS
Clean the outside of the pan with commercial oven cleaner. Let set for 2 hours and the accumulated black stains can be removed with vinegar and water.

CAN OPENER
Loosen grime by brushing with an old toothbrush. To thoroughly clean blades, run a paper towel through the cutting process.

ENAMELWARE CASSEROLE DISHES
Fill a dish that contains stuck food bits with boiling water and 2 T. of baking soda. Let it stand and wash out.

DISHES
Save time and money by using the cheapest brand of dishwashing detergent available, but add a few tablespoons of vinegar to the dishwasher. The vinegar will cut the grease and leave your dishes sparkling clean.

Before washing fine china and crystal, place a towel on the bottom of the sink to act as a cushion.

To remove coffee or tea stains and cigarette burns from fine china, rub with a damp cloth dipped in baking soda.

DISHWASHER
Run a cup of white vinegar through the entire cycle in an empty dishwasher to remove all soap film.

CLOGGED DRAINS
When a drain is clogged with grease, pour a cup of salt and a cup of baking soda into the drain followed by a kettle of boiling water. The grease will usually dissolve immediately and open the drain.

Coffee grounds are a no-no. They do a nice job of clogging, especially if they get mixed with grease.

GARBAGE DISPOSAL
Grind a half lemon or orange rind in the disposal to remove any unpleasant odor.

OVEN
Following a spill, sprinkle with salt immediately. When oven is cool, brush off burnt food and wipe with a damp sponge.

Sprinkle bottom of oven with automatic dishwasher soap and cover with wet paper towels. Let stand for a few hours.

A quick way to clean oven parts is to place a bath towel in the bathtub and pile all removable parts from the oven onto it. Draw enough hot water to just cover the parts and sprinkle a cup of dishwasher soap over it. While you are cleaning the inside of the oven, the rest will be cleaning itself.

An inexpensive oven cleaner. Set oven on warm for about 20 minutes, then turn off. Place a small dish of full strength ammonia on the top shelf. Put large pan of boiling water on the bottom shelf and let it set overnight. In the morning, open oven and let it air a while before washing off with soap and water. Even the hard baked-on grease will wash off easily.

PLASTIC CUPS, DISHES AND CONTAINERS

Coffee or tea stains can be scoured with baking soda.

Or, fill the stained cup with hot water and drop in a few denture cleanser tablets. Let soak for 1 hour.

To rid foul odors from plastic containers, place crumbled-up newspaper (black and white only) into the container. Cover tightly and leave overnight.

REFRIGERATOR

To help eliminate odors fill a small bowl with charcoal (the kind used for potted plants) and place it on a shelf in the refrigerator. It absorbs ordors rapidly.

An open box of baking soda will absorb food odors for at least a month or two.

A little vanilla poured on a piece of cotton and place in the refrigerator will eliminate odors.

To prevent mildew from forming, wipe with vinegar. The acid effectively kills the mildew fungus.

Use a glycerine-soaked cloth to wipe sides and shelves. Future spills wipe up easily. Add after the freezer has been defrosted, coat the inside coils with glycerine. The next time you defrost, the ice will loosen quickly and drop off in sheets.

Wash inside and out with a mixture of 3 T. of baking soda in a quart of warm water.

SINKS

For a sparkling white sink, place paper towels across the bottom of your sink and saturate with household bleach. Let set for ½ hour or so.

Rub stainless steel sinks with lighter fluid if rust marks appear. After the rust disappears, wipe with your regular kitchen cleanser.

Use a cloth dampened with rubbing alcohol to remove water spots from stainless steel.

Spots on stainless steel can also be removed with white vinegar.

Club soda will shine up stainless steel sinks in a jiffy.

SPONGES
Wash in your dishwasher or soak overnight in salt water or baking soda added to water.

THERMOS BOTTLE
Fill the bottle with warm water, add 1 tsp. of baking soda and allow to soak.

TIN PIE PANS
Remove rust by dipping a raw potato in cleaning powder and scouring.

FINGERPRINTS OFF THE KITCHEN DOOR AND WALLS
Take away fingerprints and grime with a solution of half water and half ammonia. Put it in a spray bottle from one of these expensive cleaning products, you'll never have to buy them again.

FORMICA TOPS
Polish them to a sparkle with club soda.

KEEPING FOODS FRESH AND FOOD STORAGE

CELERY AND LETTUCE
Store in refrigerator in paper bags instead of plastic. Leave the outside leaves and stalks on until ready to use.

ONIONS
Once an onion has been cut in half, rub the leftover side with butter and it will keep fresh longer.

CHEESE
Wrap cheese in a vinegar-dampened cloth to keep it from drying out.

MILK
Milk at room temperature may spoil cold milk, so don't pour milk back into the carton.

BROWN SUGAR
Wrap in a plastic bag and store in refrigerator in a coffee can with a snap-on lid.

COCOA
Store cocoa in a glass jar in a dry and cool place.

CAKES
Putting half an apple in the cake box will keep cake moist.

ICE CREAM
Ice cream that has been opened and returned to the freezer sometimes forms a waxlike film on the top. To prevent this, after part of the ice cream has been removed press a piece of waxed paper against the surface and reseal the carton.

LEMONS
Store whole lemons in a tightly sealed jar of water in the refrigerator. They will yield much more juice than when first purchased.

LIMES
Store limes, wrapped in tissue paper, on lower shelf of the refrigerator.

SMOKED MEATS
Wrap ham or bacon in vinegar-soaked cloth, then in waxed paper to preserve freshness.

STRAWBERRIES
Keep in a colander in the refrigerator. Wash just before serving.

(Continued on Next Page)

MISSISSIPPI RIVER PO' FOLK
by Pat Wallace . . . . paperback $9.95

STRANGE FOLKS ALONG THE MISSISSIPPI
by Pat Wallace . . . . paperback $9.95

THE VANISHING OUTHOUSE OF IOWA
by Bruce Carlson . . . . paperback $9.95

THE VANISHING OUTHOUSE OF ILLINOIS
by Bruce Carlson . . . . paperback $9.95

THE VANISHING OUTHOUSE OF MINNESOTA
by Bruce Carlson . . . . paperback $9.95

THE VANISHING OUTHOUSE OF WISCONSIN
by Bruce Carlson . . . . paperback $9.95

MISSISSIPPI RIVER COOKIN' BOOK
by Bruce Carlson . . . . paperback $11.95

IOWA'S ROAD KILL COOKBOOK
by Bruce Carlson . . . . paperback $7.95

HITCH HIKING THE UPPER MIDWEST
by Bruce Carlson . . . . paperback $7.95

IOWA, THE LAND BETWEEN THE VOWELS
by Bruce Carlson . . . . paperback $9.95
(Farm Boy Stories from the Early 1900's)

GHOSTS OF SOUTHWEST MINNESOTA
by Ruth Hein . . . . paperback $9.95

ME 'N WESLEY
by Bruce Carlson . . . . paperback $9.95
*(Stories about the homemade toys that farm children
made and played with around the turn of the century.)*

SOUTH DAKOTA ROAD KILL COOKBOOK
by Bruce Carlson . . . . paperback $7.95

Some Pretty Tame, But Kinda Funny Stories About Early DAKOTA LADIES-OF-THE-EVENING
by Bruce Carlson ....paperback $9.95

Some Pretty Tame, But Kinda Funny Stories About Early IOWA LADIES-OF-THE EVENING
by Bruce Carlson ....paperback $9.95

Some Pretty Tame, But Kinda Funny Stories About Early ILLINOIS LADIES-OF-THE-EVENING
by Bruce Carlson ....paperback $9.95

Some Pretty Tame, But Kinda Funny Stories About Early MINNESOTA LADIES-OF-THE-EVENING
by Bruce Carlson ....paperback $9.95

Some Pretty Tame, But Kinda Funny Stories About Early WISCONSIN LADIES-OF-THE-EVENING
by Bruce Carlson ....paperback $9.95

THE DAKOTA'S VANISHING OUTHOUSE
by Bruce Carlson ....paperback $9.95

ILLINOIS' ROAD KILL COOKBOOK
by Bruce Carlson ....paperback $7.95

OLD IOWA HOUSES, YOUNG LOVES
by Bruce Carlson ....paperback $9.95
(Stories about old houses in Iowa and young love they have known.)

TERROR IN THE BLACK HILLS
by Dick Kennedy ....paperback $9.95

IOWA'S EARLY HOME REMEDIES
by various...paperback $9.95

GHOSTS OF DOOR COUNTY, WISCONSIN
by Geri Rider ....paperback $9.95

THE VANISHING OUTHOUSE OF MISSOURI
by Bruce Carlson ....paperback $9.95

JACK KING vs. DETECTIVE MacKENZIE
by N. Bell ....paperback $9.95

RIVER SHARKS & SHENANIGANS
by N. Bell . . . . paperback $9.95
(Tales of Riverboat Gambling of Years Ago)

TALES OF HACKETT'S CREEK
by D. Titus . . . . paperback $9.95
(1940's Miss. River Kids)

ROMANCE ON BOARD
by Helen Colby . . . . paperback $9.95

UNSOLVED MYSTERIES OF THE MISSISSIPPI
by N. Bell . . . . paperback $9.95

TALL TALES OF THE MISSOURI RIVER
by D. Titus . . . . paperback $9.95

MAKIN' DO IN SOUTH DAKOTA
by various. . . . . paperback $9.95

TRICKS WE PLAYED IN IOWA
by various. . . . . paperback $9.95

CHILDREN OF THE RIVER
by various. . . . . paperback $9.95

LET'S GO DOWN IN THE RIVER 'AN . . .
by various. . . . . paperback $9.95

EARLY WISCONSIN HOME REMEDIES
by various. . . . . paperback $9.95

EARLY MISSOURI HOME REMEDIES
by various. . . . . paperback $9.95

MY VERY FIRST . . .
by various. . . . . paperback $9.95

101 WAYS FOR MIDWESTERNERS TO "DO IN THEIR NEIGHBOR'S PESKY DOG WITHOUT GETTING CAUGHT
by B. Carlson . . . . paperback $5.95

SOUTH DAKOTA ROADKILL COOKBOOK
by B. Carlson . . . . paperback $7.95

A FIELD GUIDE TO IOWA'S CRITTERS
by B. Carlson .... paperback $7.95

A FIELD GUIDE TO MISSOURI'S CRITTERS
by B. Carlson .... paperback $7.95

MISSOURI'S ROADKILL COOKBOOK
by B. Carlson .... paperback $7.95

A FIELD GUIDE TO ILLINOIS' CRITTERS
by B. Carlson .... paperback $7.95

MINNESOTA'S ROADKILL COOKBOOK
by B. Carlson .... paperback $7.95

REVENGE OF THE ROADKILL
by B. Carlson .... paperback $7.95

THE MOTORIST'S FIELD GUIDE TO MIDWEST FARM EQUIPMENT
by B. Carlson .... paperback $5.95
(Misguided Information as only a City Slicker can get it Messed Up)

ILLINOIS EARLY HOME REMEDIES
by various .... paperback $9.95

GUNSHOOTIN', WHISKEY DRINKIN', GIRL CHASIN' TALES OUT OF THE OLD DAKOTA TERRITORY
by Netha Bell .... paperback $9.95

WYOMING'S ROADKILL COOKBOOK
by B. Carlson .... paperback $7.95

MONTANA'S ROADKILL COOKBOOK
by B. Carlson .... paperback $7.95

SHE CRIED WITH HER BOOTS ON
by M. Walsh .... paperback $9.95
(Tales of an Early Nebraska Housewife)

SKUNK RIVER ANTHOLOGY
by Gene "Will" Olson .... paperback $9.95

101 WAYS TO USE A DEAD RIVER FLY
by B. Carlson .... paperback $7.95

FUNNER THINGS TO DO COOKBOOK
by Louise Lum .... paperback $11.95

MAKIN'-DO IN ILLINOIS
by various.. paperback $9.95

OLD MISSOURI HOUSES, NEW LOVES
by Bruce Carlson .... paperback $9.95

YOU KNOW YOU'RE IN IOWA WHEN . . .
by Bruce Carlson .... paperback $7.95